www.EffortlessMath.com

... So Much More Online!

- ✓ FREE Math lessons
- ✓ More Math learning books!
- ✓ Mathematics Worksheets
- ✓ Online Math Tutors

Need a PDF version of this book?

Please visit www.EffortlessMath.com

GED Mathematical Reasoning Prep 2020-2021

The Most Comprehensive Review and Ultimate Guide to the GED Math Test

By

Reza Nazari & Ava Ross

All inquiries should be addressed to:

info@effortlessMath.com

www.EffortlessMath.com

ISBN: 978-1-64612-198-4

Published by: Effortless Math Education

www.EffortlessMath.com

Description

GED Mathematical Reasoning Prep 2020 – 2021, which reflects the 2020 - 2021 test guidelines, is dedicated to preparing test takers to ace the GED Math Test. This comprehensive GED Math Prep book with hundreds of examples, abundant sample GED mathematics questions, and two full-length and realistic GED Math tests is all you will ever need to fully prepare for the GED Math. It will help you learn everything you need to ace the math section of the GED test.

Effortless Math unique study program provides you with an in-depth focus on the math portion of the exam, helping you master the math skills that students find the most troublesome. This GED Math preparation book contains most common sample questions that are most likely to appear in the mathematics section of the GED.

Inside the pages of this comprehensive GED Math book, students can learn basic math operations in a structured manner with a complete study program to help them understand essential math skills. It also has many exciting features, including:

- ✓ Content 100% aligned with the 2020 - 2021 GED test
- ✓ Written by GED Math instructors and test experts
- ✓ Complete coverage of all GED Math concepts and topics which you will be tested
- ✓ Numerous GED math practice questions in both multiple-choice and grid-in formats with answers grouped by topic, so you can focus on your weak areas
- ✓ Abundant Math skill building exercises to help test-takers approach different question types that might be *unfamiliar* to them
- ✓ Exercises on different GED Math topics such as integers, percent, equations, polynomials, exponents and radicals
- ✓ 2 full-length practice tests (featuring new question types) with detailed answers

GED Mathematical Reasoning Prep 2020 – 2021 is an incredibly useful resource for those who want to review all topics being covered on the GED test. It efficiently and effectively reinforces learning outcomes through engaging questions and repeated practice, helping you to quickly master Math skills.

About the Author

Reza Nazari is the author of more than 100 Math learning books including:
– **Math and Critical Thinking Challenges:** For the Middle and High School Student
– **ACT Math in 30 Days**
– **ASVAB Math Workbook 2018 - 2019**
– **Effortless Math Education Workbooks**
– **and many more Mathematics books ...**

Reza is also an experienced Math instructor and a test–prep expert who has been tutoring students since 2008. Reza is the founder of Effortless Math Education, a tutoring company that has helped many students raise their standardized test scores—and attend the colleges of their dreams. Reza provides an individualized custom learning plan and the personalized attention that makes a difference in how students view math.

You can contact Reza via email at:
reza@EffortlessMath.com

Find Reza's professional profile at:
goo.gl/zoC9rJ

Chapter 1:

Fractions and Mixed Numbers

Math Topics that you'll learn in this Chapter:

- ✓ Simplifying Fractions
- ✓ Adding and Subtracting Fractions
- ✓ Multiplying and Dividing Fractions
- ✓ Adding Mixed Numbers
- ✓ Subtracting Mixed Numbers
- ✓ Multiplying Mixed Numbers
- ✓ Dividing Mixed Numbers

Simplifying Fractions

- A fraction contains two numbers separated by a bar in between them. The bottom number, called the denominator, is the total number of equally divided portions in one whole. The top number, called the numerator, is how many portions you have. And the bar represents the operation of division.
- Simplifying a fraction means reducing it to lowest terms. To simplify a fraction, evenly divide both the top and bottom of the fraction by $2, 3, 5, 7, \ldots$ etc.
- Continue until you can't go any further.

Examples:

1) Simplify $\frac{12}{30}$

Solution: To simplify $\frac{12}{30}$, find a number that both 12 and 30 are divisible by.

Both are divisible by 6. Then: $\frac{12}{30} = \frac{12 \div 6}{30 \div 6} = \frac{2}{5}$

2) Simplify $\frac{64}{80}$

Solution: To simplify $\frac{64}{80}$, find a number that both 64 and 80 are divisible by.

Both are divisible by 8 and 16. Then: $\frac{64}{80} = \frac{64 \div 8}{80 \div 8} = \frac{8}{10}$, 8 and 10 are divisible by 2,

then: $\frac{8}{10} = \frac{4}{5}$ or $\frac{64}{80} = \frac{64 \div 16}{80 \div 16} = \frac{4}{5}$

3) Simplify $\frac{20}{60}$

Solution: To simplify $\frac{20}{60}$, find a number that both 20 and 60 are divisible by. Both are divisible by 20.

Then: $\frac{20}{60} = \frac{20 \div 20}{60 \div 20} = \frac{1}{3}$

Adding and Subtracting Fractions

- For "like" fractions (fractions with the same denominator), add or subtract the numerators (top numbers) and write the answer over the common denominator (bottom numbers).
- Adding and Subtracting fractions with the same denominator:

$$\frac{a}{b}+\frac{c}{b}=\frac{a+c}{b} \qquad \frac{a}{b}-\frac{c}{b}=\frac{a-c}{b}$$

- Find equivalent fractions with the same denominator before you can add or subtract fractions with different denominators.
- Adding and Subtracting fractions with different denominators:

$$\frac{a}{b}+\frac{c}{d}=\frac{ad+bc}{bd} \qquad \frac{a}{b}-\frac{c}{d}=\frac{ad-bc}{bd}$$

Examples:

1) Find the sum. $\frac{3}{4}+\frac{1}{3}=$

Solution: These two fractions are "unlike" fractions. (they have different denominators). Use this formula: $\frac{a}{b}+\frac{c}{d}=\frac{ad+cb}{bd}$

Then: $\frac{3}{4}+\frac{1}{3}=\frac{(3)(3)+(4)(1)}{4\times 3}=\frac{9+4}{12}=\frac{13}{12}$

2) Find the difference. $\frac{4}{5}-\frac{3}{7}=$

Solution: For "unlike" fractions, find equivalent fractions with the same denominator before you can add or subtract fractions with different denominators. Use this formula:

$\frac{a}{b}-\frac{c}{d}=\frac{ad-bc}{bd}$

$\frac{4}{5}-\frac{3}{7}=\frac{(4)(7)-(3)(5)}{5\times 7}=\frac{28-15}{35}=\frac{13}{35}$

Multiplying and Dividing Fractions

- Multiplying fractions: multiply the top numbers and multiply the bottom numbers.

  Simplify if necessary. $\frac{a}{b} \times \frac{c}{d} = \frac{a \times c}{b \times d}$

- Dividing fractions: Keep, Change, Flip

  Keep first fraction, change division sign to multiplication, and flip the numerator and denominator of the second fraction. Then, solve! $\frac{a}{b} \div \frac{c}{d} = \frac{a}{b} \times \frac{d}{c} = \frac{a \times d}{b \times c}$

Examples:

1) Multiply. $\frac{5}{8} \times \frac{2}{3} =$

   Solution: Multiply the top numbers and multiply the bottom numbers.

   $\frac{5}{8} \times \frac{2}{3} = \frac{5 \times 2}{8 \times 3} = \frac{10}{24}$, simplify: $\frac{10}{24} = \frac{10 \div 2}{24 \div 2} = \frac{5}{12}$

2) Solve. $\frac{1}{3} \div \frac{4}{7} =$

   Solution: Keep first fraction, change division sign to multiplication, and flip the numerator and denominator of the second fraction.

   Then: $\frac{1}{3} \div \frac{4}{7} = \frac{1}{3} \times \frac{7}{4} = \frac{1 \times 7}{3 \times 4} = \frac{7}{12}$

3) Calculate. $\frac{3}{5} \times \frac{2}{3} =$

   Solution: Multiply the top numbers and multiply the bottom numbers.

   $\frac{3}{5} \times \frac{2}{3} = \frac{3 \times 2}{5 \times 3} = \frac{6}{15}$, simplify: $\frac{6}{15} = \frac{6 \div 3}{15 \div 3} = \frac{2}{5}$

4) Solve. $\frac{1}{4} \div \frac{5}{6} =$

   Solution: Keep first fraction, change division sign to multiplication, and flip the numerator and denominator of the second fraction.

   Then: $\frac{1}{4} \div \frac{5}{6} = \frac{1}{4} \times \frac{6}{5} = \frac{1 \times 6}{4 \times 5} = \frac{6}{20}$, simplify: $\frac{6}{20} = \frac{6 \div 2}{20 \div 2} = \frac{3}{10}$

Adding Mixed Numbers

Use following steps for adding mixed numbers:

- Add whole numbers of the mixed numbers.
- Add the fractions of the mixed numbers.
- Find the Least Common Denominator (LCD) if necessary.
- Add whole numbers and fractions.
- Write your answer in lowest terms.

Examples:

1) Add mixed numbers. $3\frac{1}{3}+1\frac{4}{5}=$

Solution: Let's rewriting our equation with parts separated, $3\frac{1}{3}+1\frac{4}{5}=3+\frac{1}{3}+1+\frac{4}{5}$. Now, add whole number parts: $3+1=4$

Add the fraction parts $\frac{1}{3}+\frac{4}{5}$. Rewrite to solve with the equivalent fractions. $\frac{1}{3}+\frac{4}{5}=\frac{5}{15}+\frac{12}{15}=\frac{17}{15}$. The answer is an improper fraction (numerator is bigger than denominator). Convert the improper fraction into a mixed number: $\frac{17}{15}=1\frac{2}{15}$. Now, combine the whole and fraction parts: $4+1\frac{2}{15}=5\frac{2}{15}$

2) Find the sum. $1\frac{2}{5}+2\frac{1}{2}=$

Solution: Rewriting our equation with parts separated, $1+\frac{2}{5}+2+\frac{1}{2}$. Add the whole number parts:

$1+2=3$. Add the fraction parts: $\frac{2}{5}+\frac{1}{2}=\frac{4}{10}+\frac{5}{10}=\frac{9}{10}$

Now, combine the whole and fraction parts: $3+\frac{9}{10}=3\frac{9}{10}$

Subtract Mixed Numbers

Use the following steps for subtracting mixed numbers.

- ✓ Convert mixed numbers into improper fractions. $a\frac{c}{b}=\frac{ab+c}{b}$
- ✓ Find equivalent fractions with the same denominator for unlike fractions. (fractions with different denominators)
- ✓ Subtract the second fraction from the first one. $\frac{a}{b}-\frac{c}{d}=\frac{ad-bc}{bd}$
- ✓ Write your answer in lowest terms.
- ✓ If the answer is an improper fraction, convert it into a mixed number.

Examples:

1) Subtract. $3\frac{4}{5}-1\frac{3}{4}=$

Solution: Convert mixed numbers into fractions: $3\frac{4}{5}=\frac{3\times5+4}{5}=\frac{19}{5}$ and $1\frac{3}{4}=\frac{1\times4+3}{4}=\frac{7}{4}$
These two fractions are "unlike" fractions. (they have different denominators). Find equivalent fractions with the same denominator. Use this formula: $\frac{a}{b}-\frac{c}{d}=\frac{ad-bc}{bd}$
$\frac{19}{5}-\frac{7}{4}=\frac{(19)(4)-(5)(7)}{5\times4}=\frac{76-35}{20}=\frac{41}{20}$, the answer is an improper fraction, convert it into a mixed number. $\frac{41}{20}=2\frac{1}{20}$

2) Subtract. $4\frac{3}{8}-1\frac{1}{2}=$

Solution: Convert mixed numbers into fractions: $4\frac{3}{8}=\frac{4\times8+3}{8}=\frac{35}{8}$ and $1\frac{1}{2}=\frac{1\times2+1}{4}=\frac{3}{2}$
Find equivalent fractions: $\frac{3}{2}=\frac{12}{8}$. Then: $4\frac{3}{8}-1\frac{1}{2}=\frac{35}{8}-\frac{12}{8}=\frac{23}{8}$
The answer is an improper fraction, convert it into a mixed number.

$$\frac{23}{8}=2\frac{7}{8}$$

Multiplying Mixed Numbers

Use following steps for multiplying mixed numbers:

- ✓ Convert the mixed numbers into fractions. $a\frac{c}{b} = a + \frac{c}{b} = \frac{ab+c}{b}$
- ✓ Multiply fractions. $\frac{a}{b} \times \frac{c}{d} = \frac{a \times c}{b \times d}$
- ✓ Write your answer in lowest terms.
- ✓ If the answer is an improper fraction (numerator is bigger than denominator), convert it into a mixed number.

Examples:

1) Multiply. $3\frac{1}{3} \times 4\frac{1}{6} =$

   Solution: Convert mixed numbers into fractions, $3\frac{1}{3} = \frac{3\times3+1}{3} = \frac{10}{3}$ and $4\frac{1}{6} = \frac{4\times6+1}{6} = \frac{25}{6}$

   Apply the fractions rule for multiplication, $\frac{10}{3} \times \frac{25}{6} = \frac{10\times25}{3\times6} = \frac{250}{18}$

   The answer is an improper fraction. Convert it into a mixed number. $\frac{250}{18} = 13\frac{8}{9}$

2) Multiply. $2\frac{1}{2} \times 3\frac{2}{3} =$

   Solution: Converting mixed numbers into fractions, $2\frac{1}{2} \times 3\frac{2}{3} = \frac{5}{2} \times \frac{11}{3}$

   Apply the fractions rule for multiplication, $\frac{5}{2} \times \frac{11}{3} = \frac{5\times11}{2\times3} = \frac{55}{6} = 9\frac{1}{6}$

3) Multiply mixed numbers. $2\frac{1}{3} \times 2\frac{1}{2} =$

   Solution: Converting mixed numbers to fractions, $2\frac{1}{3} = \frac{7}{3}$ and $2\frac{1}{2} = \frac{5}{2}$. Multiply two fractions:

$$\frac{7}{3} \times \frac{5}{2} = \frac{7 \times 5}{3 \times 2} = \frac{35}{6} = 5\frac{5}{6}$$

Dividing Mixed Numbers

Use following steps for dividing mixed numbers:

- Convert the mixed numbers into fractions. $a\frac{c}{b} = a + \frac{c}{b} = \frac{ab + c}{b}$
- Divide fractions: Keep, Change, Flip: Keep first fraction, change division sign to multiplication, and flip the numerator and denominator of the second fraction. Then, solve! $\frac{a}{b} \div \frac{c}{d} = \frac{a}{b} \times \frac{d}{c} = \frac{a \times d}{b \times c}$
- Write your answer in lowest terms.
- If the answer is an improper fraction (numerator is bigger than denominator), convert it into a mixed number.

Examples:

1) Solve. $3\frac{2}{3} \div 2\frac{1}{2}$

Solution: Convert mixed numbers into fractions: $3\frac{2}{3} = \frac{3\times3+2}{3} = \frac{11}{3}$ and $2\frac{1}{2} = \frac{2\times2+1}{2} = \frac{5}{2}$

Keep, Change, Flip: $\frac{11}{3} \div \frac{5}{2} = \frac{11}{3} \times \frac{2}{5} = \frac{11\times2}{3\times5} = \frac{22}{15}$. The answer is an improper fraction. Convert it into a mixed number: $\frac{22}{15} = 1\frac{7}{15}$

2) Solve. $3\frac{4}{5} \div 1\frac{5}{6}$

Solution: Convert mixed numbers to fractions, then solve:

$$3\frac{4}{5} \div 1\frac{5}{6} = \frac{19}{5} \div \frac{11}{6} = \frac{19}{5} \times \frac{6}{11} = \frac{114}{55} = 2\frac{4}{55}$$

3) Solve. $2\frac{2}{7} \div 2\frac{3}{5}$

Solution: Converting mixed numbers to fractions: $3\frac{4}{5} \div 1\frac{5}{6} = \frac{16}{7} \div \frac{13}{5}$

Keep, Change, Flip: $\frac{16}{7} \div \frac{13}{5} = \frac{16}{7} \times \frac{5}{13} = \frac{16\times5}{7\times13} = \frac{80}{91}$

Chapter 1: Practices

Simplify each fraction.

1) $\frac{18}{30} =$

2) $\frac{21}{42} =$

3) $\frac{35}{55} =$

4) $\frac{48}{72} =$

5) $\frac{54}{81} =$

6) $\frac{80}{200} =$

Find the sum or difference.

7) $\frac{6}{15} + \frac{3}{15} =$

8) $\frac{2}{3} + \frac{1}{9} =$

9) $\frac{1}{4} + \frac{2}{5} =$

10) $\frac{7}{10} - \frac{3}{10} =$

11) $\frac{1}{2} - \frac{3}{8} =$

12) $\frac{5}{7} - \frac{3}{5} =$

Find the answers.

13) $\frac{1}{7} \div \frac{3}{8} =$

14) $\frac{2}{3} \times \frac{4}{7} =$

15) $\frac{5}{7} \times \frac{3}{4} =$

16) $\frac{2}{5} \div \frac{3}{7} =$

17) $\frac{3}{7} \div \frac{5}{8} =$

18) $\frac{3}{8} \times \frac{4}{7} =$

Calculate.

19) $3\frac{1}{5} + 2\frac{2}{9} =$

20) $1\frac{1}{7} + 5\frac{2}{5} =$

21) $4\frac{4}{5} + 1\frac{2}{7} =$

22) $2\frac{4}{7} + 2\frac{3}{5} =$

23) $1\frac{5}{6} + 1\frac{2}{5} =$

24) $3\frac{5}{7} + 1\frac{2}{9} =$

Calculate.

25) $3\frac{2}{5} - 1\frac{2}{9} =$

26) $5\frac{3}{5} - 1\frac{1}{7} =$

27) $4\frac{2}{5} - 2\frac{2}{7} =$

28) $8\frac{3}{4} - 2\frac{1}{8} =$

29) $9\frac{5}{7} - 7\frac{4}{21} =$

30) $11\frac{7}{12} - 9\frac{5}{6} =$

Find the answers.

31) $1\frac{1}{8} \times 1\frac{3}{4} =$

32) $3\frac{1}{5} \times 2\frac{2}{7} =$

33) $2\frac{1}{8} \times 1\frac{2}{9} =$

34) $2\frac{3}{8} \times 2\frac{2}{5} =$

35) $1\frac{1}{2} \times 5\frac{2}{3} =$

36) $3\frac{1}{2} \times 6\frac{2}{3} =$

Solve.

37) $9\frac{1}{2} \div 2\frac{3}{5} =$

38) $2\frac{3}{8} \div 1\frac{2}{5} =$

39) $5\frac{3}{4} \div 2\frac{2}{7} =$

40) $8\frac{1}{3} \div 4\frac{1}{4} =$

41) $7\frac{2}{5} \div 3\frac{3}{4} =$

42) $2\frac{4}{5} \div 3\frac{2}{3} =$

Answers – Chapter 1

1) $\frac{3}{5}$
2) $\frac{1}{2}$
3) $\frac{7}{11}$
4) $\frac{2}{3}$
5) $\frac{2}{3}$
6) $\frac{2}{5}$
7) $\frac{3}{5}$
8) $\frac{7}{9}$
9) $\frac{13}{20}$
10) $\frac{2}{5}$
11) $\frac{1}{8}$
12) $\frac{4}{35}$
13) $\frac{8}{21}$
14) $\frac{8}{21}$
15) $\frac{15}{28}$
16) $\frac{14}{15}$
17) $\frac{24}{35}$
18) $\frac{3}{14}$
19) $5\frac{19}{45}$
20) $6\frac{19}{35}$
21) $6\frac{3}{35}$
22) $5\frac{6}{35}$
23) $3\frac{7}{30}$
24) $4\frac{59}{63}$
25) $2\frac{8}{45}$
26) $6\frac{16}{35}$
27) $2\frac{4}{35}$
28) $6\frac{5}{8}$
29) $2\frac{11}{21}$
30) $1\frac{3}{4}$
31) $1\frac{31}{32}$
32) $7\frac{11}{35}$
33) $2\frac{43}{72}$
34) $5\frac{7}{10}$
35) $8\frac{1}{2}$
36) $23\frac{1}{3}$
37) $3\frac{17}{26}$
38) $1\frac{39}{56}$
39) $2\frac{33}{64}$
40) $1\frac{49}{51}$
41) $1\frac{73}{75}$
42) $\frac{42}{55}$

Chapter 2:

Decimals

Math Topics that you'll learn in this Chapter:

- ✓ Comparing Decimals
- ✓ Rounding Decimals
- ✓ Adding and Subtracting Decimals
- ✓ Multiplying and Dividing Decimals

Comparing Decimals

- Decimal is a fraction written in a special form. For example, instead of writing $\frac{1}{2}$ you can write 0.5
- A Decimal Number contains a Decimal Point. It separates the whole number part from the fractional part of a decimal number.
- Let's review decimal place values: Example: 53.9861

5: tens	3: ones	9: tenths
8: hundredths	6: thousandths	1: tens thousandths

✅ To compare decimals, compare each digit of two decimals in the same place value. Start from left. Compare hundreds, tens, ones, tenth, hundredth, etc.

✅ To compare numbers, use these symbols:

Equal to $=$, Less than $<$, Greater than $>$

Greater than or equal $\geq$, Less than or equal $\leq$

Examples:

1) Compare 0.60 and 0.06.

Solution: 0.60 *is greater than* 0.06, because the tenth place of 0.60 is 6, but the tenth place of 0.06 is zero. Then: $0.60 > 0.06$

2) Compare 0.0815 and 0.815.

Solution: 0.815 *is greater than* 0.0815, because the tenth place of 0.815 is 8, but the tenth place of 0.0815 is zero. Then: $0.0815 < 0.815$

Rounding Decimals

- We can round decimals to a certain accuracy or number of decimal places. This is used to make calculation easier to do and results easier to understand, when exact values are not too important.
- First, you'll need to remember your place values: For example:

$$12.4869$$

1: tens	2: ones	4: tenths
8: hundredths	6: thousandths	9: tens thousandths

- To round a decimal, first find the place value you'll round to.
- Find the digit to the right of the place value you're rounding to. If it is 5 or bigger, add 1 to the place value you're rounding to and remove all digits on its right side. If the digit to the right of the place value is less than 5, keep the place value and remove all digits on the right.

Examples:

1) Round 1.9278 to the thousandth place value.

Solution: First look at the next place value to the right, (tens thousandths). It's 8 and it is greater than 5. Thus add 1 to the digit in the thousandth place. Thousandth place is 7. → $7 + 1 = 8$, then, the answer is 1.928

2) Round 9.4126 to the nearest hundredth.

Solution: First look at the digit to the right of hundredth (thousandths place value). It's 2 and it is less than 5, thus remove all the digits to the right of hundredth place. Then, the answer is 9.41

Adding and Subtracting Decimals

- Line up the decimal numbers.
- Add zeros to have same number of digits for both numbers if necessary.
- Remember your place values: For example:

73.5196

7: tens	3: ones	5: tenths
1: hundredths	9: thousandths	6: tens thousandths

- Add or subtract using column addition or subtraction.

Examples:

1) Add. $1.8 + 3.12$

Solution: First line up the numbers: $\begin{array}{r} 1.8 \\ +3.12 \\ \hline \end{array}$ → Add a zero to have same number of digits for both numbers. $\begin{array}{r} 1.80 \\ +3.12 \\ \hline \end{array}$ → Start with the hundredths place: $0 + 2 = 2$, $\begin{array}{r} 1.80 \\ +3.12 \\ \hline 2 \end{array}$ → Continue with tenths place: $8 + 1 = 9$, $\begin{array}{r} 1.80 \\ +3.12 \\ \hline .92 \end{array}$ → Add the ones place: $3 + 1 = 4$, $\begin{array}{r} 1.80 \\ +3.12 \\ \hline 4.92 \end{array}$

2) Find the difference. $3.67 - 2.23$

Solution: First line up the numbers: $\begin{array}{r} 3.67 \\ -2.23 \\ \hline \end{array}$ → Start with the hundredths place: $7 - 3 = 4$, $\begin{array}{r} 3.67 \\ -2.23 \\ \hline 4 \end{array}$ → Continue with tenths place. $6 - 2 = 4$, $\begin{array}{r} 3.67 \\ -2.23 \\ \hline .44 \end{array}$ → Subtract the ones place. $3 - 2 = 1$, $\begin{array}{r} 3.67 \\ -2.23 \\ \hline 1.44 \end{array}$

Multiplying and Dividing Decimals

For multiplying decimals:

- ✓ Ignore the decimal point and set up and multiply the numbers as you do with whole numbers.
- ✓ Count the total number of decimal places in both of the factors.
- ✓ Place the decimal point in the product.

For dividing decimals:

- ✓ If the divisor is not a whole number, move decimal point to right to make it a whole number. Do the same for dividend.
- ✓ Divide similar to whole numbers.

Examples:

1) Find the product. $0.81 \times 0.32 =$

Solution: Set up and multiply the numbers as you do with whole numbers. Line up the numbers: $\frac{81}{\times 32}$ → Start with the ones place then continue with other digits → $\frac{\begin{array}{r}81\\ \times 32\end{array}}{2{,}592}$. Count the total number of decimal places in both of the factors. There are four decimals digits. (two for each factor 0.81 and 0.32) Then: $0.81 \times 0.32 = 0.2592$

2) Find the quotient. $1.60 \div 0.4 =$

Solution: The divisor is not a whole number. Multiply it by 10 to get 4: → $0.4 \times 10 = 4$

Do the same for the dividend to get 16. → $1.60 \times 10 = 1.6$

Now, divide: $16 \div 4 = 4$. The answer is 4.

Chapter 2: Practices

Compare. Use $>$, $=$, and $<$

1) $0.88 \square 0.088$
2) $0.56 \square 0.57$
3) $0.99 \square 0.89$
4) $1.55 \square 1.65$
5) $1.58 \square 1.75$
6) $2.91 \square 2.85$

Round each decimal to the nearest whole number.

7) 5.94
8) 16.47
9) 9.7
10) 35.8
11) 24.46
12) 12.5

Find the sum or difference.

13) $43.15 + 23.65 =$
14) $56.74 - 22.43 =$
15) $25.47 + 31.76 =$
16) $69.87 - 35.98 =$
17) $45.53 + 18.95 =$
18) $25.13 - 18.72 =$

Find the product and quotient.

19) $0.5 \times 0.8 =$
20) $6.4 \div 0.4 =$
21) $3.25 \times 2.2 =$
22) $8.4 \div 2.5 =$
23) $5.4 \times 0.6 =$
24) $1.42 \div 0.5 =$

Answers – Chapter 2

1) $0.88 > 0.088$
2) $0.56 < 0.57$
3) $0.99 > 0.89$
4) $1.55 < 1.65$
5) $1.58 < 1.75$
6) $2.91 > 2.85$
7) 6
8) 16
9) 10
10) 36
11) 24
12) 13
13) 66.8
14) 34.31
15) 57.23
16) 33.89
17) 64.48
18) 6.41
19) 0.4
20) 16
21) 7.15
22) 3.36
23) 3.24
24) 2.84

Chapter 3: Integers and Order of Operations

Math Topics that you'll learn in this Chapter:

- ✓ Adding and Subtracting Integers
- ✓ Multiplying and Dividing Integers
- ✓ Order of Operations
- ✓ Integers and Absolute Value

Adding and Subtracting Integers

- Integers include: zero, counting numbers, and the negative of the counting numbers. $\{\ldots, -3, -2, -1, 0, 1, 2, 3, \ldots\}$
- Add a positive integer by moving to the right on the number line. (you will get a bigger number)
- Add a negative integer by moving to the left on the number line. (you will get a smaller number)
- Subtract an integer by adding its opposite.

Examples:

1) Solve. $(-4) - (-5) =$

   Solution: Keep the first number and convert the sign of the second number to its opposite. (change subtraction into addition. Then: $(-4) + 5 = 1$

2) Solve. $11 + (8 - 19) =$

   Solution: First subtract the numbers in brackets, $8 - 19 = -11$.

   Then: $11 + (-11) =$ → change addition into subtraction: $11 - 11 = 0$

3) Solve. $5 - (-14 - 3) =$

   Solution: First subtract the numbers in brackets, $-14 - 3 = -17$

   Then: $5 - (-17) =$ → change subtraction into addition: $5 + 17 = 22$

4) Solve. $10 + (-6 - 15) =$

   Solution: First subtract the numbers in brackets, $-6 - 15 = -21$

   Then: $10 + (-21) =$ → change addition into subtraction: $10 - 21 = -11$

Multiplying and Dividing Integers

Use following rules for multiplying and dividing integers:

- ✓ (negative) × (negative) = positive
- ✓ (negative) ÷ (negative) = positive
- ✓ (negative) × (positive) = negative
- ✓ (negative) ÷ (positive) = negative
- ✓ (positive) × (positive) = positive
- ✓ (positive) ÷ (negative) = negative

Examples:

1) Solve. $2 \times (-3) =$

Solution: Use this rule: (positive) × (negative) = negative.
Then: $(2) \times (-3) = -6$

2) Solve. $(-5) + (-27 \div 9) =$

Solution: First divided -27 by 9 , the numbers in brackets, use this rule:
(negative) ÷ (positive) = negative. Then: $-27 \div 9 = -3$
$(-5) + (-27 \div 9) = (-5) + (-3) = -5 - 3 = -8$

3) Solve. $(15 - 17) \times (-8) =$

Solution: First subtract the numbers in brackets, $15 - 17 = -2 \rightarrow (-2) \times (-8) =$

Now use this rule: (negative) × (negative) = positive
$(-2) \times (-8) = 16$

4) Solve. $(16 - 10) \div (-2) =$

Solution: First subtract the numbers in brackets, $16 - 10 = 6 \rightarrow (6) \div (-2) =$

Now use this rule: (positive) ÷ (negative) = negative
$(6) \div (-2) = -3$

Order of Operations

- In Mathematics, "operations" are addition, subtraction, multiplication, division, exponentiation (written as b^n), and grouping;
- When there is more than one math operation in an expression, use PEMDAS: (to memorize this rule, remember the phrase "Please Excuse My Dear Aunt Sally".)
  - Parentheses
  - Exponents
  - Multiplication and Division (from left to right)
  - Addition and Subtraction (from left to right)

Examples:

1) Calculate. $(3+5) \div (3^2 \div 9) =$

   Solution: First simplify inside parentheses: $(8) \div (9 \div 9) = (8) \div (1)$, Then: $(8) \div (1) = 8$

2) Solve. $(7 \times 8) - (12 - 4) =$

   Solution: First calculate within parentheses: $(7 \times 8) - (12 - 4) = (56) - (8)$, Then: $(56) - (8) = 48$

3) Calculate. $-2[(8 \times 9) \div (2^2 \times 2)] =$

   Solution: First calculate within parentheses: $-2[(72) \div (4 \times 2)] = -2[(72) \div (8)] = -2[9]$ multiply -2 and 9. Then: $-2[9] = -18$

4) Solve. $(14 \div 7) + (-13 + 8) =$

   Solution: First calculate within parentheses: $(14 \div 7) + (-13 + 8) = (2) + (-5)$

   Then: $(2) - (5) = -3$

Integers and Absolute Value

- The absolute value of a number is its distance from zero, in either direction, on the number line. For example, the distance of 9 and -9 from zero on number line is 9.
- The absolute value of an integer is the numerical value without its sign. (negative or positive)
- The vertical bar is used for absolute value as in $|x|$.
- The absolute value of a number is never negative; because it only shows, "how far the number is from zero".

Examples:

1) Calculate. $|12 - 4| \times 4 =$

Solution: First solve $|12 - 4|$, →$|12 - 4| = |8|$, the absolute value of 8 is 8, $|8| = 8$

Then: $8 \times 4 = 32$

2) Solve. $\frac{|-16|}{4} \times |3 - 8| =$

Solution: First find $|-16|$, → the absolute value of -16 is 16, then: $|-16| = 16$,

$\frac{16}{4} \times |3 - 8| =$

Now, calculate $|3 - 8|$, → $|3 - 8| = |-5|$, the absolute value of -5 is 5. $|-5| = 5$

Then: $\frac{16}{4} \times 5 = 4 \times 5 = 20$

3) Solve. $|9 - 3| \times \frac{|-3\times8|}{6} =$

Solution: First calculate $|9 - 3|$, →$|9 - 3| = |6|$, the absolute value of 6 is 6, $|6| = 6$. Then:

$6 \times \frac{|-3\times8|}{6}$

Now calculate $|-3 \times 8|$, → $|-3 \times 8| = |-24|$, the absolute value of -24 is 24, $|-24| = 24$

Then: $6 \times \frac{24}{6} = 6 \times 4 = 24$

Chapter 3: Practices

Find each sum or difference.

1) $18 + (-5) =$
2) $(-16) + 24 =$
3) $(-12) + (-9) =$
4) $14 + (-8) + 6 =$
5) $24 + (-10 - 7) =$
6) $(-15) + (-6 + 12) =$

Find each product or quotient.

7) $8 \times (-6) =$
8) $(-12) \div (-3) =$
9) $(-4) \times (-7) \times 2 =$
10) $3 \times (-5) \times (-6) =$
11) $(-7 - 37) \div (-11) =$
12) $(8 - 6) \times (-24) =$

Evaluate each expression.

13) $8 + (3 \times 7) =$
14) $(18 \times 2) - 14 =$
15) $(15 - 7) + (2 \times 6) =$
16) $(8 + 4) \div (2^3 \div 2) =$
17) $2[(6 \times 3) \div (3^2 \times 2)] =$
18) $-3[(8 \times 2^2) \div (8 \times 2)] =$

Find the answers.

19) $|-6| + |9 - 12| =$
20) $|8| - |7 - 19| + 1 =$
21) $\frac{|-40|}{8} \times \frac{|-15|}{5} =$
22) $|7 \times -5| \times \frac{|-32|}{8} =$
23) $\frac{|-121|}{11} - |-8 \times 2| =$
24) $\frac{|-3 \times -6|}{9} \times \frac{|4 \times -6|}{8} =$

Answers – Chapter 3

1) 13
2) 8
3) -21
4) 12
5) 7
6) -9
7) -48
8) 4
9) 56
10) 90
11) 4
12) -48
13) 29
14) 22
15) 20
16) 3
17) 2
18) -6
19) 9
20) -3
21) 15
22) 140
23) -5
24) 6

Chapter 4:

Ratios and Proportions

Math Topics that you'll learn in this Chapter:

- ✓ Simplifying Ratios
- ✓ Proportional Ratios
- ✓ Similarity and Ratios

Simplifying Ratios

- Ratios are used to make comparisons between two numbers.
- Ratios can be written as a fraction, using the word "to", or with a colon.
  Example: $\frac{3}{4}$ or "3 to 4" or 3:4
- You can calculate equivalent ratios by multiplying or dividing both sides of the ratio by the same number.

Examples:

1) Simplify. $9:3 =$

   Solution: Both numbers 9 and 3 are divisible by 3 , $\Rightarrow 9 \div 3 = 3, \quad 3 \div 3 = 1$, Then: $9:3 = 3:1$

2) Simplify. $\frac{24}{44} =$

   Solution: Both numbers 24 and 44 are divisible by 4, $\Rightarrow 24 \div 4 = 6, 44 \div 4 = 11$, Then: $\frac{24}{44} = \frac{6}{11}$

3) There are 36 students in a class and 16 of them are girls. Write the ratio of girls to boys.

   Solution: Subtract 16 from 36 to find the number of boys in the class. $36 - 16 = 20$. There are 20 boys in the class. So, ratio of girls to boys is $16:20$. Now, simplify this ratio. Both 20 and 16 are divisible by 4. Then: $20 \div 4 = 5$, and $16 \div 4 = 4$. In simplest form, this ratio is $4:5$

4) A recipe calls for butter and sugar in the ratio $3:4$. If you're using 9 cups of butter, how many cups of sugar should you use?

   Solution: Since, you use 9 cups of butter, or 3 times as much, you need to multiply the amount of sugar by 3. Then: $4 \times 3 = 12$. So, you need to use 12 cups of sugar. You can solve this using equivalent fractions: $\frac{3}{4} = \frac{9}{12}$

Proportional Ratios

- Two ratios are proportional if they represent the same relationship.
- A proportion means that two ratios are equal. It can be written in two ways: $\frac{a}{b} = \frac{c}{d}$ $\quad a : b = c : d$
- The proportion $\frac{a}{b} = \frac{c}{d}$ can be written as: $a \times d = c \times b$

Examples:

1) Solve this proportion for x. $\frac{3}{7} = \frac{12}{x}$

Solution: Use cross multiplication: $\frac{3}{7} = \frac{12}{x} \Rightarrow 3 \times x = 7 \times 12 \Rightarrow 3x = 84$

Divide both sides by 3 to find x: $x = \frac{84}{3} \Rightarrow x = 28$

2) If a box contains red and blue balls in ratio of $3: 7$ red to blue, how many red balls are there if 49 blue balls are in the box?

Solution: Write a proportion and solve. $\frac{3}{7} = \frac{x}{49}$

Use cross multiplication: $3 \times 49 = 7 \times x \Rightarrow 147 = 7x$

Divide to find x: $x = \frac{147}{7} \Rightarrow x = 21$. There are 21 red balls in the box.

3) Solve this proportion for x. $\frac{2}{9} = \frac{12}{x}$

Solution: Use cross multiplication: $\frac{2}{9} = \frac{12}{x} \Rightarrow 2 \times x = 9 \times 12 \Rightarrow 2x = 108$

Divide to find x: $x = \frac{108}{2} \Rightarrow x = 54$

4) Solve this proportion for x. $\frac{6}{7} = \frac{18}{x}$

Solution: Use cross multiplication: $\frac{6}{7} = \frac{18}{x} \Rightarrow 6 \times x = 7 \times 18 \Rightarrow 6x = 126$

Divide to find x: $x = \frac{126}{6} \Rightarrow x = 21$

Similarity and Ratios

- Two figures are similar if they have the same shape.
- Two or more figures are similar if the corresponding angles are equal, and the corresponding sides are in proportion.

Examples:

1) Following triangles are similar. What is the value of unknown side?

Solution: Find the corresponding sides and write a proportion.

$\frac{5}{10} = \frac{4}{x}$. Now, use cross product to solve for x:

$\frac{5}{10} = \frac{4}{x} \rightarrow 5 \times x = 10 \times 4 \rightarrow 5x = 40$. Divide both sides by 5. Then: $5x = 40 \rightarrow \frac{5x}{5} = \frac{40}{5} \rightarrow x = 8$

The missing side is 8.

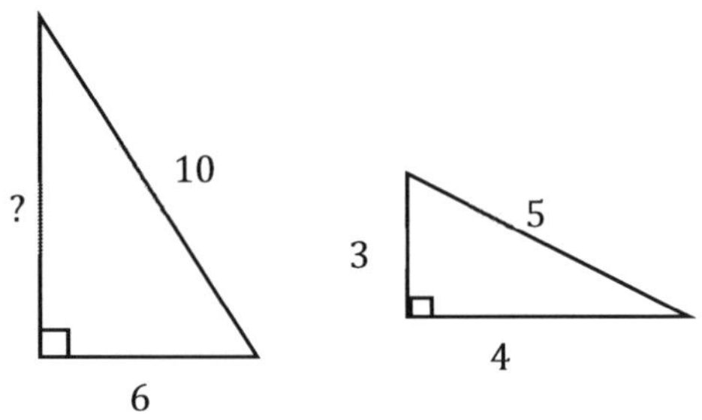

2) Two rectangles are similar. The first is 6 feet wide and 20 feet long. The second is 15 feet wide. What is the length of the second rectangle?

Solution: Let's put x for the length of the second rectangle. Since two rectangles are similar, their corresponding sides are in proportion. Write a proportion and solve for the missing number. $\frac{6}{15} = \frac{20}{x} \rightarrow 6x = 15 \times 20 \rightarrow 6x = 300 \rightarrow x = \frac{300}{6} = 50$

The length of the second rectangle is 50 feet.

Chapter 4: Practices

Reduce each ratio.

1) $9:18 =$ ___:___
2) $6:54 =$ ___:___
3) $28:49 =$ ___:___
4) Bob has 12 red cards and 20 green cards. What is the ratio of Bob's red cards to his green cards? ________________

5) In a party, 10 soft drinks are required for every 12 guests. If there are 252 guests, how many soft drinks is required? ________________

6) In Jack's class, 18 of the students are tall and 10 are short. In Michael's class 54 students are tall and 30 students are short. Which class has a higher ratio of tall to short students? ________________

Solve each proportion.

7) $\frac{3}{7} = \frac{18}{x}, x =$ ____
8) $\frac{5}{9} = \frac{x}{108}, x =$ ____
9) $\frac{2}{13} = \frac{8}{x}, x =$ ____
10) $\frac{4}{10} = \frac{6}{x}, x =$ ____
11) $\frac{8}{20} = \frac{x}{65}, x =$ ____
12) $\frac{6}{15} = \frac{14}{x}, x =$ ____

Solve each problem.

13) Two rectangles are similar. The first is $8\,feet$ wide and $22\,feet$ long. The second is $12\,feet$ wide. What is the length of the second rectangle? ________________

14) Two rectangles are similar. One is $3.2\,meters$ by $8\,meters$. The longer side of the second rectangle is $34.5\,meters$. What is the other side of the second rectangle? ________________

Answers – Chapter 4

1) 1: 2
2) 1: 9
3) 4: 7
4) 3: 5
5) 210
6) The ratio for both classes is 9 to 5.
7) 42
8) 60
9) 52
10) 15
11) 26
12) 35
13) 33 feet
14) 13.8 meters

Chapter 5:

Percentage

Math Topics that you'll learn in this Chapter:

- ✓ Percentage Calculations
- ✓ Percent Problems
- ✓ Percent of Increase and Decrease
- ✓ Discount, Tax and Tip
- ✓ Simple Interest

Percent Problems

- Percent is a ratio of a number and 100. It always has the same denominator, 100. Percent symbol is "%".
- Percent means "per 100". So, 20% is 20/100.
- In each percent problem, we are looking for the base, or part or the percent.
- Use the following equations to find each missing section in a percent problem:
  - Base = Part ÷ Percent
  - Part = Percent × Base
  - Percent = Part ÷ Base

Examples:

1) What is 25% of 60?

Solution: In this problem, we have percent (25%) and base (60) and we are looking for the "part".

Use this formula: $part = percent \times base$. Then: $part = 25\% \times 60 = \frac{25}{100} \times 60 = 0.25 \times 60 = 15$.

The answer:

25% of 60 is 15.

2) 20 is what percent of 400?

Solution: In this problem, we are looking for the percent. Use this equation:

$$Percent = Part \div Base \rightarrow Percent = 20 \div 400 = 0.05 = 5\%.$$

Then: 20 is 5 percent of 400.

Percent of Increase and Decrease

- Percent of change (increase or decrease) is a mathematical concept that represents the degree of change over time.
- To find the percentage of increase or decrease:

1. New Number - Original Number
2. The result ÷ Original Number × 100

- Or use this formula: Percent of change = $\frac{new\ number - original\ number}{original\ number} \times 100$
- Note: If your answer is a negative number, then this is a percentage decrease. If it is positive, then this is a percentage increase.

Examples:

1) The price of a shirt increases from $\$20$ to $\$30$. What is the percentage increase?
Solution: First find the difference: $30 - 20 = 10$
Then: $10 \div 20 \times 100 = \frac{10}{20} \times 100 = 50$. The percentage increase is 50. It means that the price of the shirt increased 50%.

2) The price of a table increased from $\$25$ to $\$40$. What is the percent of increase?
Solution: Use percentage formula: $Percent\ of\ change = \frac{new\ number - original\ number}{original\ number} \times 100 = \frac{40-25}{25} \times 100 = \frac{15}{25} \times 100 = 0.6 \times 100 = 60$. The percentage increase is 60. It means that the price of the table increased 60%.

3) The population of a town was 50,000 in the 2000 census and 40,000 in the 2010 census. By what percent did the population decrease?
Solution: Use percentage formula:
$Percent\ of\ change = \frac{new\ number - original\ number}{original\ number} \times 100 = \frac{40{,}000 - 50{,}000}{50{,}000} \times 100 = \frac{-10{,}000}{50{,}000} \times 100 = -0.2 \times 100 = -20$. The population of the town decreased by 20%.

Discount, Tax and Tip

- To find discount: Multiply the regular price by the rate of discount
- To find selling price: Original price – discount
- To find tax: Multiply the tax rate to the taxable amount (income, property value, etc.)
- To find tip, multiply the rate to the selling price.

Examples:

1) With an 10% discount, Ella was able to save $\$45$ on a dress. What was the original price of the dress?

   Solution: let x be the original price of the dress. Then: $10\ \%\ of\ x = 45$. Write an equation and solve for x: $0.10 \times x = 45 \rightarrow x = \frac{45}{0.10} = 450$. The original price of the dress was \$450.

2) Sophia purchased a new computer for a price of \$950 at the Apple Store. What is the total amount her credit card is charged if the sales tax is 7%?

   Solution: The taxable amount is \$950, and the tax rate is 7%. Then: $Tax = 0.07 \times 950 = 66.50$

   $Final\ price = Selling\ price + Tax \rightarrow final\ price = \$950 + \$66.50 = \$1{,}016.50$

3) Nicole and her friends went out to eat at a restaurant. If their bill was \$80.00 and they gave their server a 15% tip, how much did they pay altogether?

   Solution: First find the tip. To find tip, multiply the rate to the bill amount.

   $Tip = 80 \times 0.15 = 12$. The final price is: $\$80 + \$12 = \$92$

Simple Interest

- Simple Interest: The charge for borrowing money or the return for lending it.
- Simple interest is calculated on the initial amount (principal).
- To solve a simple interest problem, use this formula:

  Interest = principal x rate x time $(\boldsymbol{I = p \times r \times t = prt})$

Examples:

1) Find simple interest for $\$300$ investment at 6% for 5 years.

   Solution: Use Interest formula: $I = prt$ ($P = \$300$, $\text{r} = 6\% = \frac{6}{100} = 0.06$ and $t = 5$)
   Then: $I = 300 \times 0.06 \times 5 = \$90$

2) Find simple interest for $\$1{,}600$ at 5% for 2 years.

   Solution: Use Interest formula: $I = prt$ ($P = \$1{,}600$, $\text{r} = 5\% = \frac{5}{100} = 0.05$ and $t = 2$)
   Then: $I = 1{,}600 \times 0.05 \times 2 = \$160$

3) Andy received a student loan to pay for his educational expenses this year. What is the interest on the loan if he borrowed $6,500 at 8% for 6 years?
   Solution: Use Interest formula: $I = prt$. $P = \$6{,}500$, $\text{r} = 8\% = 0.08$ and $t = 6$

   Then: $I = 6{,}500 \times 0.08 \times 8 = \$3{,}120$

4) Bob is starting his own small business. He borrowed $10,000 from the bank at a 6% rate for 6 months. Find the interest Bob will pay on this loan.
   Solution: Use Interest formula: $I = prt$. $P = \$10{,}000$, $\text{r} = 6\% = 0.06$ and $t = 0.5$ (6 months is half year). Then: $I = 10{,}000 \times 0.06 \times 0.5 = \$300$

Chapter 5: Practices

Solve each problem.

1) 15 is what percent of 60? ____%
2) 18 is what percent of 24? ____%
3) 25 is what percent of 500? ____%
4) 14 is what percent of 280? ____%
5) 45 is what percent of 180? ____%
6) 70 is what percent of 350? ____%

Solve each percent of change word problem.

7) Bob got a raise, and his hourly wage increased from $15 to $18. What is the percent increase? ______ %
8) The price of a pair of shoes increases from $40 to $66. What is the percent increase? ____ %
9) At a coffeeshop, the price of a cup of coffee increased from $1.20 to $1.44. What is the percent increase in the cost of the coffee? ______ %

Find the selling price of each item.

10)Original price of a computer: $650

Tax: 8%, Selling price: $________

11) Original price of a laptop: $480

Tax: 15%, Selling price: $________

12) Nicolas hired a moving company. The company charged $400 for its services, and Nicolas gives the movers a 15% tip. How much does Nicolas tip the movers? $__________

13) Mason has lunch at a restaurant and the cost of his meal is $30. Mason wants to leave a 20% tip. What is Mason's total bill including tip? $__________

Determine the simple interest for these loans.

14) $\$440\ at\ 5\%\ for\ 6\ years.$ $__

15) $\$460\ at\ 2.5\%\ for\ 4\ years.$ $_

16) $\$500\ at\ 3\%\ for\ 5\ years.$ $__

17) $550 at 9% for 2 years. $__

18) A new car, valued at $28,000, depreciates at 9% per year. What is the value of the car one year after purchase? $______________

19) Sara puts $4,000 into an investment yielding 5% annual simple interest; she left the money in for five years. How much interest does Sara get at the end of those five years? $______________

Answers – Chapter 5

1) 25%
2) 75%
3) 5%
4) 5%
5) 25%
6) 20%
7) 20%
8) 65%
9) 20%
10) $702.00
11) $552.00
12) $60.00
13) $36.00
14) $132
15) $46
16) $75
17) $99
18) $25,480.00
19) $1,000.00

Chapter 6:

Expressions and Variables

Math Topics that you'll learn in this Chapter:

- ✓ Simplifying Variable Expressions
- ✓ Simplifying Polynomial Expressions
- ✓ The Distributive Property
- ✓ Evaluating One Variable
- ✓ Evaluating Two Variables

Simplifying Variable Expressions

- In algebra, a variable is a letter used to stand for a number. The most common letters are: $x, y, z, a, b, c, m, and\ n$.
- Algebraic expression is an expression contains integers, variables, and the math operations such as addition, subtraction, multiplication, division, etc.
- In an expression, we can combine "like" terms. (values with same variable and same power)

Examples:

1) Simplify. $(2x + 3x + 4) =$

Solution: In this expression, there are three terms: $2x, 3x$, and 4. Two terms are "like terms": $2x$ and $3x$. Combine like terms. $2x + 3x = 5x$. Then: $(2x + 3x + 4) = 5x + 4$ (remember you cannot combine variables and numbers.)

2) Simplify. $12 - 3x^2 + 5x + 4x^2 =$

Solution: Combine "like" terms: $-3x^2 + 4x^2 = x^2$. Then:

$12 - 3x^2 + 5x + 4x^2 = 12 + x^2 + 5x$. Write in standard form (biggest powers first):

$12 + x^2 + 5x = x^2 + 5x + 12$

3) Simplify. $(10x^2 + 2x^2 + 3x) =$

Solution: Combine like terms. Then: $(10x^2 + 2x^2 + 3x) = 12x^2 + 3x$

4) Simplify. $15x - 3x^2 + 9x + 5x^2 =$

Solution: Combine "like" terms: $15x + 9x = 24x$, and $-3x^2 + 5x^2 = 2x^2$

Then: $15x - 3x^2 + 9x + 5x^2 = 24x + 2x^2$. Write in standard form (biggest powers first): $24x + 2x^2 = 2x^2 + 24x$

Simplifying Polynomial Expressions

- In mathematics, a polynomial is an expression consisting of variables and coefficients that involves only the operations of addition, subtraction, multiplication, and non-negative integer exponents of variables. $P(x) = a_n x^n + a_{n-1} x^{n-1} + \ldots + a_2 x^2 + a_1 x + a_0$
- Polynomials must always be simplified as much as possible. It means you must add together any like terms. (values with same variable and same power)

Examples:

1) Simplify this Polynomial Expressions. $x^2 - 5x^3 + 2x^4 - 4x^3$

   Solution: Combine "like" terms: $-5x^3 - 4x^3 = -9x^3$

   Then: $x^2 - 5x^3 + 2x^4 - 4x^3 = x^2 - 9x^3 + 2x^4$

   Now, write the expression in standard form: $2x^4 - 9x^3 + x^2$

2) Simplify this expression. $(2x^2 - x^3) - (x^3 - 4x^2) =$

   Solution: First use distributive property: → multiply $(-)$ into $(x^3 - 4x^2)$

   $(2x^2 - x^3) - (x^3 - 4x^2) = 2x^2 - x^3 - x^3 + 4x^2$

   Then combine "like" terms: $2x^2 - x^3 - x^3 + 4x^2 = 6x^2 - 2x^3$

   And write in standard form: $6x^2 - 2x^3 = -2x^3 + 6x^2$

3) Simplify. $4x^4 - 5x^3 + 15x^4 - 12x^3 =$

   Solution: Combine "like" terms: $-5x^3 - 12x^3 = -17x^3$ and $4x^4 + 15x^4 = 19x^4$

   Then: $4x^4 - 5x^3 + 15x^4 - 12x^3 = 19x^4 - 17x^3$

The Distributive Property

- The distributive property (or the distributive property of multiplication over addition and subtraction) simplifies and solves expressions in the form of: $a(b+c)$ or $a(b-c)$
- The distributive property is multiplying a term outside the parentheses by the terms inside.
- Distributive Property rule: $a(b+c)=ab+ac$

Examples:

1) *Simply using distributive property.* $(-4)(x-5)$

   Solution: Use Distributive Property rule: $a(b+c)=ab+ac$

   $(-4)(x-5)=(-4\times x)+(-4)\times(-5)=-4x+20$

2) *Simply.* $(3)(2x-4)$

   Solution: Use Distributive Property rule: $a(b+c)=ab+ac$

   $(3)(2x-4)=(3\times 2x)+(3)\times(-4)=6x-12$

3) *Simply.* $(-3)(3x-5)+4x$

   Solution: First, simplify $(-3)(3x-5)$ using distributive property.

   Then: $(-3)(3x-5)=-9x+15$

   Now combine like terms: $(-3)(3x-5)+4x=-9x+15+4x$

   In this expression, $-9x$ and $4x$ are "like terms" and we can combine them.

   $-9x+4x=-5x$. Then: $-9x+15+4x=-5x+15$

Evaluating One Variable

- To evaluate one variable expressions, find the variable and substitute a number for that variable.
- Perform the arithmetic operations.

Examples:

1) *Calculate this expression for* $x = 3$. $15 - 3x$

Solution: First substitute 3 for x

Then: $15 - 3x = 15 - 3(3)$

Now, use order of operation to find the answer: $15 - 3(3) = 15 - 9 = 6$

2) *Evaluate this expression for* $x = 1$. $5x - 12$

Solution: First substitute 1 for x, then:

$5x - 12 = 5(1) - 12$

Now, use order of operation to find the answer: $5(1) - 12 = 5 - 12 = -7$

3) *Find the value of this expression when* $x = 5$. $25 - 4x$

Solution: First substitute 5 for x, then:

$25 - 4x = 25 - 4(5) = 25 - 20 = 5$

4) *Solve this expression for* $x = -2$. $12 + 3x$

Solution: Substitute -2 for x, then: $12 + 3x = 12 + 3(-2) = 12 - 6 = 6$

Evaluating Two Variables

- To evaluate an algebraic expression, substitute a number for each variable.
- Perform the arithmetic operations to find the value of the expression.

Examples:

1) *Calculate this expression for* a $= 3$ *and* $b = -2.\ 3a - 6b$

Solution: First substitute 3 for a, and -2 for b , then:

$$3a - 6b = 3(3) - 6(-2)$$

Now, use order of operation to find the answer: $3(3) - 6(-2) = 9 + 12 = 21$

2) *Evaluate this expression for* x $= 3$ *and* $y = 1.\quad 3x + 5y$

Solution: Substitute 3 for x, and 1 for y , then:

$$3x + 5y = 3(3) + 5(1) = 9 + 5 = 14$$

3) *Find the value of this expression when* $a = 1$ *and* $b = 2.\ 5(3a - 2b)$

Solution: Substitute 1 for a, and 2 for b , then:

$$5(3a - 2b) = 15a - 10b = 15(1) - 10(2) = 15 - 20 = -5$$

4) *Solve this expression.* $4x - 3y,\ x = 3,\ y = 5$

Solution: Substitute 3 for x, and 5 for y and simplify. Then: $4x - 3y = 4(3) - 3(5) = 12 - 15 = -3$

Chapter 6: Practices

Simplify each expression.

1) $(6x - 4x + 8 + 6) =$

2) $(-14x + 26x - 12) =$

3) $(24x - 6 - 18x + 3) =$

4) $5 + 8x^2 - 9 =$

5) $7x - 4x^2 + 6x =$

6) $15x^2 - 3x - 6x^2 + 4 =$

Simplify each polynomial.

7) $2x^2 + 5x^3 - 7x^2 + 12x =$ ________________________

8) $2x^4 - 5x^5 + 8x^4 - 8x^2 =$ ________________________

9) $5x^3 + 15x - x^2 - 2x^3 =$ ________________________

10) $(8x^3 - 6x^2) + (9x^2 - 10x) =$ ________________________

11) $(12x^4 + 4x^3) - (8x^3 - 2x^4) =$ ________________________

12) $(9x^5 - 7x^3) - (5x^3 + x^2) =$ ________________________

Use the distributive property to simply each expression.

13) $4(5 + 6x) =$

14) $5(8 - 4x) =$

15) $(-6)(2 - 9x) =$

16) $(-7)(6x - 4) =$

17) $(3x + 12)4 =$

18) $(8x - 5)(-3) =$

Evaluate each expression using the value given.

19) $8 - x, x = -3$

20) $x + 12, x = -6$

21) $5x - 3, x = 2$

22) $4 - 6x, x = 1$

23) $3x + 1, x = -2$

24) $15 - 2x, x = 5$

Evaluate each expression using the values given.

25) $4x - 2y,\ x = 4, y = -2$

26) $6a + 3b,\ a = 2, b = 4$

27) $12x - 5y - 8,\ x = 2, y = 3$

28) $-7a + 3b + 9,\ a = 4, b = 6$

29) $2x + 14 + 4y,\ x = 6, y = 8$

30) $4a - (5a - b) + 5, a = 4, b = 6$

Answers – Chapter 6

1) $2x + 14$
2) $12x - 12$
3) $6x - 3$
4) $8x^2 - 4$
5) $-4x^2 + 13x$
6) $9x^2 - 3x + 4$

7) $5x^3 - 5x^2 + 12x$
8) $-5x^5 + 10x^4 - 8x^2$
9) $3x^3 - x^2 + 15x$

10) $8x^3 + 3x^2 - 10x$
11) $14x^4 - 4x^3$
12) $9x^5 - 12x^3 - x^2$

13) $24x + 20$
14) $-20x + 40$
15) $54x - 12$
16) $-42x + 28$
17) $12x + 48$
18) $-24x + 15$

19) 11
20) 6
21) 7
22) -2
23) -5
24) 5

25) 20
26) 24
27) 1
28) -1
29) 58
30) 7

Chapter 7:

Equations and Inequalities

Math Topics that you'll learn in this Chapter:

- ✓ One–Step Equations
- ✓ Multi–Step Equations
- ✓ System of Equations
- ✓ Graphing Single–Variable Inequalities
- ✓ One–Step Inequalities
- ✓ Multi–Step Inequalities

One–Step Equations

- The values of two expressions on both sides of an equation are equal. Example: $ax = b$. In this equation, ax is equal to b.
- Solving an equation means finding the value of the variable.
- You only need to perform one Math operation in order to solve the one-step equations.
- To solve one-step equation, find the inverse (opposite) operation is being performed.
- The inverse operations are:

- Addition and subtraction
- Multiplication and division

Examples:

1) *Solve this equation for* x. $3x = 18, x = ?$

   Solution: Here, the operation is multiplication (variable x is multiplied by 3) and its inverse operation is division. To solve this equation, divide both sides of equation by 3:

   $3x = 18 \rightarrow \frac{3x}{3} = \frac{18}{3} \rightarrow x = 6$

2) *Solve this equation.* $x + 15 = 0\ ,\ x = ?$

   Solution: In this equation 15 is added to the variable x. The inverse operation of addition is subtraction. To solve this equation, subtract 15 from both sides of the equation:

   $x + 15 - 15 = 0 - 15$. Then simplify: $x + 15 - 15 = 0 - 15 \rightarrow x = -15$

3) *Solve this equation for* x. $x - 23 = 0$

   Solution: Here, the operation is subtraction and its inverse operation is addition. To solve this equation, add 23 to both sides of the equation: $x + 23 - 23 = 0 - 23 \rightarrow x = -23$

Multi–Step Equations

- To solve a multi-step equation, combine "like" terms on one side.
- Bring variables to one side by adding or subtracting.
- Simplify using the inverse of addition or subtraction.
- Simplify further by using the inverse of multiplication or division.
- Check your solution by plugging the value of the variable into the original equation.

Examples:

1) *Solve this equation for x.* $3x + 6 = 16 - 2x$

Solution: First bring variables to one side by adding $2x$ to both sides. Then:

$3x + 6 = 16 - 2x \rightarrow 3x + 6 + 2x = 16 - 2x + 2x$. Simplify: $5x + 6 = 16$

Now, subtract 6 from both sides of the equation: $5x + 6 - 6 = 16 - 6 \rightarrow 5x = 10 \rightarrow$

Divide both sides by 5: $5x = 10 \rightarrow \frac{5x}{5} = \frac{10}{5} \rightarrow x = 2$

Let's check this solution by substituting the value of 2 for x in the original equation:

$$x = 2 \rightarrow 3x + 6 = 16 - 2x \rightarrow 3(2) + 6 = 16 - 2(2) \rightarrow 6 + 6 = 16 - 4 \rightarrow 12 = 12$$

The answer $x = 2$ is correct.

2) *Solve this equation for x.* $-4x + 4 = 16$

Solution: Subtract 4 from both sides of the equation. $-4x + 4 - 4 = 16 - 4 \rightarrow -4x = 12$

Divide both sides by -4, then: $-4x = 12 \rightarrow \frac{-4x}{-4} = \frac{12}{-4} \rightarrow x = -3$

Now, check the solution: $x = -3 \rightarrow -4x + 4 = 16 \rightarrow -4(-3) + 4 = 16 \rightarrow 16 = 16$

The answer $x = -2$ is correct.

System of Equations

- A system of equations contains two equations and two variables. For example, consider the system of equations: $x - y = 1, x + y = 5$
- The easiest way to solve a system of equations is using the elimination method. The elimination method uses the addition property of equality. You can add the same value to each side of an equation.
- For the first equation above, you can add $x + y$ to the left side and 5 to the right side of the first equation: $x - y + (x + y) = 1 + 5$. Now, if you simplify, you get: $x - y + (x + y) = 1 + 5 \rightarrow 2x = 6 \rightarrow x = 3$. Now, substitute 3 for the x in the first equation: $3 - y = 1$. By solving this equation, $y = 2$

Example:

What is the value of $x + y$ *in this system of equations?* $\begin{cases} x + 2y = 6 \\ 2x - y = -8 \end{cases}$

Solution: Solving a System of Equations by Elimination:

Multiply the first equation by (-2), then add it to the second equation.

$$\frac{\begin{array}{r} -2(x + 2y = 6) \\ 2x - y = -8 \end{array}}{} \Rightarrow \begin{array}{r} -2x - 4y = -12 \\ 2x - y = -8 \end{array} \Rightarrow -5y = -20 \Rightarrow y = 4$$

Plug in the value of y into one of the equations and solve for x.

$x + 2(4) = 6 \Rightarrow x + 8 = 6 \Rightarrow x = 6 - 8 \Rightarrow x = -2$

Thus, $x + y = -2 + 4 = 2$

Graphing Single–Variable Inequalities

- An inequality compares two expressions using an inequality sign.
- Inequality signs are: "less than" $<$, "greater than" $>$, "less than or equal to" $\leq$, and "greater than or equal to" $\geq$.
- To graph a single-variable inequality, find the value of the inequality on the number line.
- For less than ($<$) or greater than ($>$) draw open circle on the value of the variable. If there is an equal sign too, then use filled circle.
- Draw an arrow to the right for greater or to the left for less than.

Examples:

1) Draw a graph for this inequality. $x > 3$

Solution: Since, the variable is greater than 3, then we need to find 3 in the number line and draw an open circle on it.

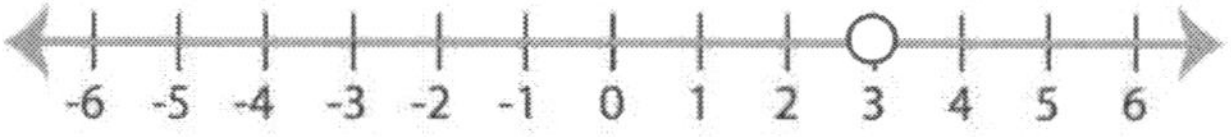

Then, draw an arrow to the right.

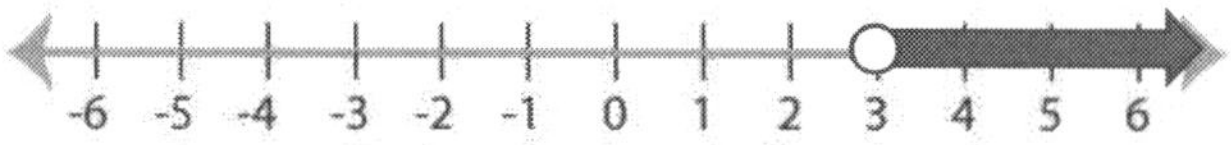

2) Graph this inequality. $x \leq -4$.

Solution: Since, the variable is less than or equal to -4, then we need to find -4 in the number line and draw a filled circle on it. Then, draw an arrow to the left.

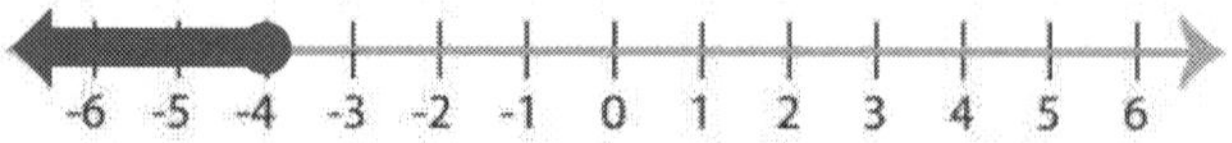

One–Step Inequalities

- An inequality compares two expressions using an inequality sign.
- Inequality signs are: "less than" $<$, "greater than" $>$, "less than or equal to" $\leq$, and "greater than or equal to" $\geq$.
- You only need to perform one Math operation in order to solve the one-step inequalities.
- To solve one-step inequalities, find the inverse (opposite) operation is being performed.
- For dividing or multiplying both sides by negative numbers, flip the direction of the inequality sign.

Examples:

1) Solve this inequality for x. $x + 3 \geq 4$

Solution: The inverse (opposite) operation of addition is subtraction. In this inequality, 3 is added to x. *To isolate* x *we need to* subtract 3 from both sides of the inequality. Then:

$x + 3 \geq 4 \rightarrow x + 3 - 3 \geq 4 - 3 \rightarrow x \geq 1$. The solution is: $x \geq 1$

2) Solve the inequality. $x - 5 > -4$.

Solution: 5 is subtracted from x. Add 5 to both sides. $x - 5 > -4 \rightarrow x - 5 + 5 > -4 + 5 \rightarrow x > 1$

3) Solve. $2x \leq -4$.

Solution: 2 is multiplied to x. Divide both sides by 2. Then: $2x \leq -4 \rightarrow \frac{2x}{2} \leq \frac{-4}{2} \rightarrow x \leq -2$

4) Solve. $-6x \leq 12$.

Solution: -6 is multiplied to x. Divide both sides by -6. Remember when dividing or multiplying both sides of an inequality by negative numbers, flip the direction of the inequality sign. Then:

$$-6x \leq 12 \rightarrow \frac{-6x}{-6} \geq \frac{12}{-6} \rightarrow x \geq -2$$

Multi–Step Inequalities

- To solve a multi-step inequality, combine "like" terms on one side.
- Bring variables to one side by adding or subtracting.
- Isolate the variable.
- Simplify using the inverse of addition or subtraction.
- Simplify further by using the inverse of multiplication or division.
- For dividing or multiplying both sides by negative numbers, flip the direction of the inequality sign.

Examples:

1) *Solve this inequality.* $2x - 3 \leq 5$

Solution: In this inequality, 3 is subtracted from $2x$. The inverse of subtraction is addition. Add 3 to both sides of the inequality: $2x - 3 + 3 \leq 5 + 3 \rightarrow 2x \leq 8$

Now, divide both sides by 2. Then: $2x \leq 8 \rightarrow \frac{2x}{2} \leq \frac{8}{2} \rightarrow x \leq 4$

The solution of this inequality is $x \leq 4$.

2) *Solve this inequality.* $3x + 9 < 12$

Solution: First subtract 9 from both sides: $3x + 9 - 9 < 12 - 9$

Then simplify: $3x + 9 - 9 < 12 - 9 \rightarrow 3x < 3$

Now divide both sides by 3: $\frac{3x}{3} < \frac{3}{3} \rightarrow x < 1$

3) *Solve this inequality.* $-2x + 4 \geq 6$

First subtract 4 from both sides: $-2x + 4 - 4 \geq 6 - 4 \rightarrow -2x \geq 2$

Divide both sides by -2. Remember that you need to flip the direction of inequality sign.

$$-2x \geq 2 \rightarrow \frac{-2x}{-2} \leq \frac{2}{-2} \rightarrow x \leq -1$$

Chapter 7: Practices

Solve each equation. (One–Step Equations)

1) $x + 7 = 6, x =$ ____

2) $8 = 2 - x, x =$ ____

3) $-10 = 8 + x, x =$ ____

4) $x - 5 = -1, x =$ ____

5) $16 = x + 9, x =$ ____

6) $12 - x = -5, x =$ ____

Solve each equation. (Multi–Step Equations)

7) $5(x + 3) = 20$

8) $-4(7 - x) = 16$

9) $8 = -2\ (x + 5)$

10) $14 = 3(4 - 2x)$

11) $5(x + 7) = -10$

12) $-2(6 + 3x) = 12$

Solve each system of equations.

13) $-5x + y = -3$ $\quad x =$

$3x - 8y = 24$ $\quad y =$

14) $3x - 2y = 2$ $\quad x =$

$x - y = 2$ $\quad y =$

15) $4x + 7y = 2$ $\quad x =$

$6x + 7y = 10$ $\quad y =$

16) $5x + 7y = 18$ $\quad x =$

$-3x + 7y = -22$ $\quad y =$

Draw a graph for each inequality.

17) $x \leq -2$

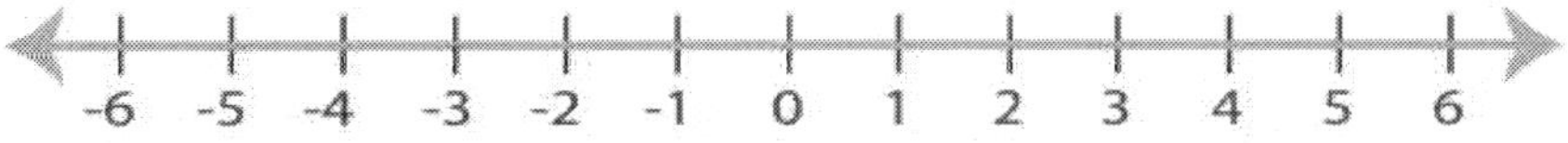

18) $x > -6$

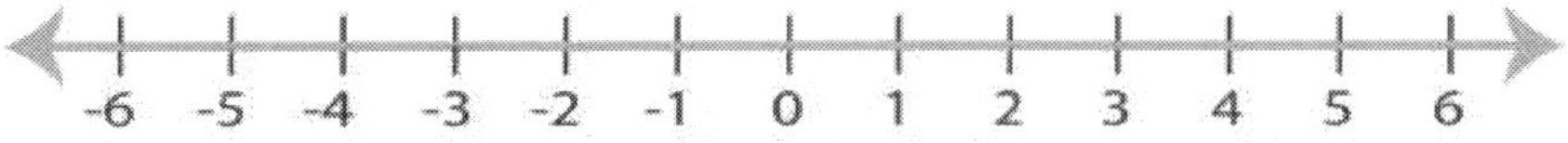

Solve each inequality and graph it.

19) $x - 3 \geq -1$

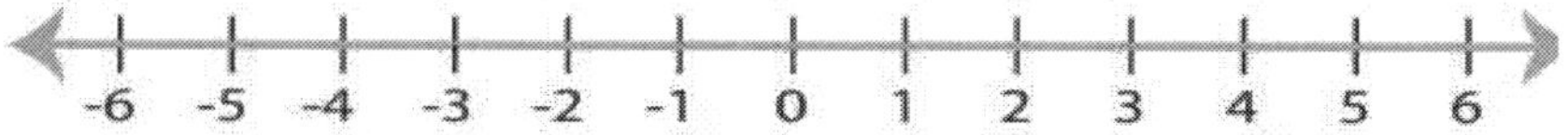

20) $3x - 2 < 16$

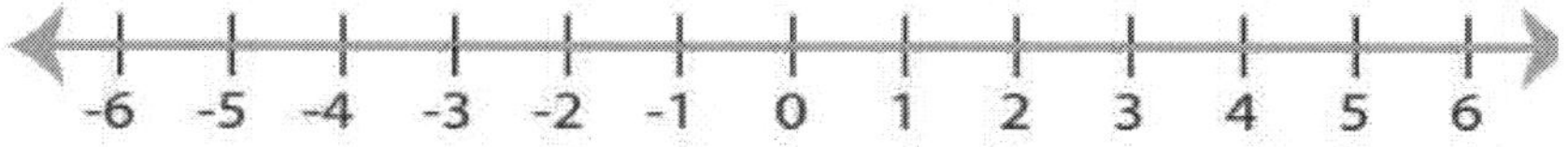

Solve each inequality.

21) $3x + 15 > -6$

22) $-18 + 4x \leq 10$

23) $4(x + 5) \geq 8$

24) $7x - 16 < 12$

25) $3(9 + x) \geq 15$

26) $-8 + 6x > 22$

Answers – Chapter 7

1) -1
2) -6
3) -18
4) 4
5) 7
6) 17

7) 1
8) 11
9) -9
10) $-\frac{1}{3}$
11) -9
12) -4

13) $x = 0\ , y = -3$

14) $x = -2, y = -4$

15) $x = 4, y = -2$

16) $x = 5, y = -1$

17) 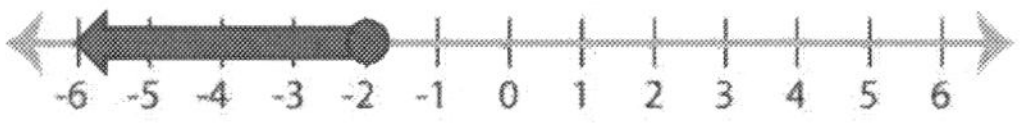

18) 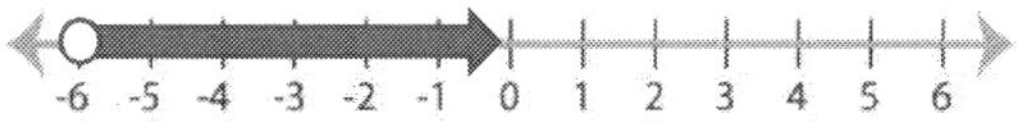

19) 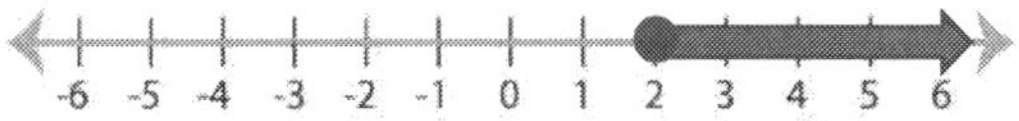

20) 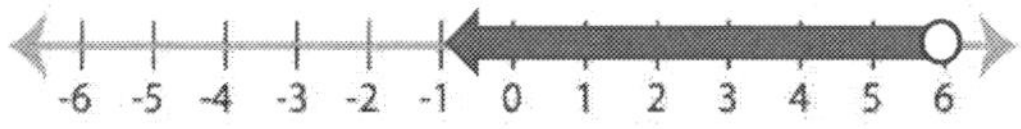

21) $x > -7$
22) $x \leq 7$
23) $x \geq -3$
24) $x < 4$
25) $x \geq -4$
26) $x > 5$

Chapter 8:

Lines and Slope

Math Topics that you'll learn in this Chapter:

- ✓ Finding Slope
- ✓ Graphing Lines Using Slope–Intercept Form
- ✓ Writing Linear Equations
- ✓ Graphing Linear Inequalities
- ✓ Finding Midpoint
- ✓ Finding Distance of Two Points

Finding Slope

- The slope of a line represents the direction of a line on the coordinate plane.
- A coordinate plane contains two perpendicular number lines. The horizontal line is x and the vertical line is y. The point at which the two axes intersect is called the origin. An ordered pair (x, y) shows the location of a point.
- A line on coordinate plane can be drawn by connecting two points.
- To find the slope of a line, we need the equation of the line or two points on the line.
- The slope of a line with two points A (x_1, y_1) and B (x_2, y_2) can be found by using this formula: $\frac{y_2 - y_1}{x_2 - x_1} = \frac{rise}{\text{run}}$
- The equation of a line is typically written as $y = mx + b$ where m is the slope and b is the y-intercept.

Examples:

1) *Find the slope of the line through these two points:* $\text{A}(2, -7)$ *and* $B(4, 3)$.

Solution: Slope $= \frac{y_2 - y_1}{x_2 - x_1}$. Let (x_1, y_1) be $\text{A}(2, -7)$ and (x_2, y_2) be $B(4, 3)$. (Remember, you can choose any point for (x_1, y_1) and (x_2, y_2)). *Then:* slope $= \frac{y_2 - y_1}{x_2 - x_1} = \frac{3-(-7)}{4-2} = \frac{10}{2} = 5$

The slope of the line through these two points is 5.

2) *Find the slope of the line with equation* $\text{y} = 3\text{x} + 6$

Solution: when the equation of a line is written in the form of $y = mx + b$, the slope is m. In this line: $y = 3x + 6$, the slope is 3.

Graphing Lines Using Slope–Intercept Form

- Slope-intercept form of a line: given the slope m and the y–intercept (the intersection of the line and y-axis) b, then the equation of the line is: $y = mx + b$
- To draw the graph of a linear equation in slope-intercept form on the xy coordinate plane, find two points on the line by plugging two values for x and calculating the values of y.
- You can also use the slope (m) and one point to graph the line.

Example:

1) *Sketch the graph of* $y = 2x - 4$.

Solution: To graph this line, we need to find two points. When x is zero the value of y is -4. And when x is 2 the value of y is 0.

$$x = 0 \rightarrow y = 2(0) - 4 = -4,$$
$$y = 0 \rightarrow 0 = 2x - 4 \rightarrow x = 2$$

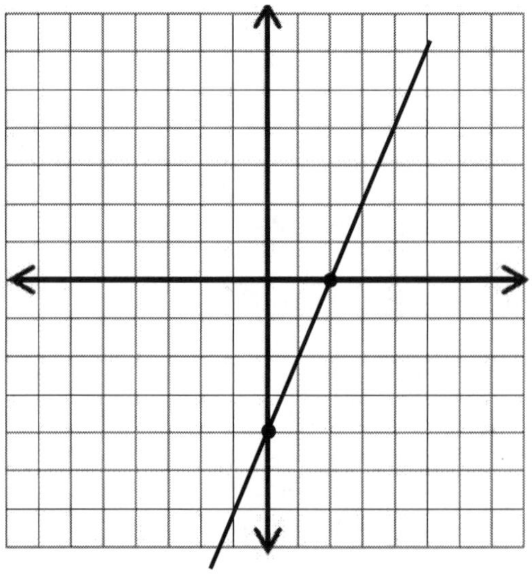

Now, we have two points: $(0, -4)$ and $(2, 0)$.

Find the points on the coordinate plane and graph the line. Remember that the slope of the line is 2.

Writing Linear Equations

- ✓ The equation of a line in slope-intercept form: $\boldsymbol{y = mx + b}$
- ✓ To write the equation of a line, first identify the slope.
- ✓ Find the y-intercept. This can be done by substituting the slope and the coordinates of a point $(\boldsymbol{x}, \boldsymbol{y})$ on the line.

Examples:

1) What is the equation of the line that passes through $(\mathbf{2}, -\mathbf{4})$ and has a slope of $\mathbf{8}$?

Solution: The general slope-intercept form of the equation of a line is $y = mx + b$, where m is the slope and b is the y-intercept.
By substitution of the given point and given slope: $y = mx + b \rightarrow -4 = (2)(8) + b$
So, $b = -4 - 16 = -20$, and the required equation is $y = 8x - 20$

2) Write the equation of the line through two points $A(2, 1)$ and $B(-2, 5)$.

Solution: Fist find the slope: $Slop = \frac{y_2 - y_1}{x_2 - x_1} = \frac{5-1}{-2-2} = \frac{4}{-4} = -1 \rightarrow m = -1$
To find the value of b, use either points and plug in the values of x and y in the equation. The answer will be the same: $y = -x + b$. Let's check both points. Then:
$(2, 1) \rightarrow y = mx + b \rightarrow 1 = -1(2) + b \rightarrow b = 3$
$(-2,5) \rightarrow y = mx + b \rightarrow 5 = -1(-2) + b \rightarrow b = 3$. The y-intercept of the line is 3.
The equation of the line is: $y = -x + 3$

3) What is the equation of the line that passes through $(\mathbf{2}, -\mathbf{1})$ and has a slope of $\mathbf{5}$?

Solution: The general slope-intercept form of the equation of a line is $y = mx + b$, where m is the slope and b is the y-intercept.
By substitution of the given point and given slope: $y = mx + b \rightarrow -1 = (5)(2) + b$
So, $b = -1 - 10 = -11$, and the equation of the line is: $y = 5x - 11$.

Finding Midpoint

- The middle of a line segment is its midpoint.
- The Midpoint of two endpoints A (x_1, y_1) and B (x_2, y_2) can be found using this formula: M $(\frac{x_1+x_2}{2}, \frac{y_1+y_2}{2})$

Examples:

1) Find the midpoint of the line segment with the given endpoints. $(\mathbf{1}, \mathbf{-3}), (\mathbf{3}, \mathbf{7})$

Solution: Midpoint $= (\frac{x_1+x_2}{2}, \frac{y_1+y_2}{2}) \rightarrow (x_1, y_1) = (1, -3)$ and $(x_2, y_2) = (3, 7)$

Midpoint $= (\frac{1+3}{2}, \frac{-3+7}{2}) \rightarrow (\frac{4}{2}, \frac{4}{2}) \rightarrow M(2, 2)$

2) Find the midpoint of the line segment with the given endpoints. $(\mathbf{-4}, \mathbf{5}), (\mathbf{8}, \mathbf{-7})$

Solution: Midpoint $= (\frac{x_1+x_2}{2}, \frac{y_1+y_2}{2}) \rightarrow (x_1, y_1) = (-4, 5)$ and $(x_2, y_2) = (8, -7)$

Midpoint $= (\frac{-4+8}{2}, \frac{5-7}{2}) \rightarrow (\frac{4}{2}, \frac{-2}{2}) \rightarrow M(2, -1)$

3) Find the midpoint of the line segment with the given endpoints. $(\mathbf{5}, \mathbf{-2}), (\mathbf{1}, \mathbf{10})$

Solution: Midpoint $= (\frac{x_1+x_2}{2}, \frac{y_1+y_2}{2}) \rightarrow (x_1, y_1) = (5, -2)$ and $(x_2, y_2) = (1,10)$

Midpoint $= (\frac{5+1}{2}, \frac{-2+10}{2}) \rightarrow (\frac{6}{2}, \frac{8}{2}) \rightarrow M(3, 4)$

4) Find the midpoint of the line segment with the given endpoints. $(\mathbf{2}, \mathbf{3}), (\mathbf{12}, \mathbf{-9})$

Solution: Midpoint $= (\frac{x_1+x_2}{2}, \frac{y_1+y_2}{2}) \rightarrow (x_1, y_1) = (2, 3)$ and $(x_2, y_2) = (12, -3)$

Midpoint $= (\frac{2+12}{2}, \frac{3-9}{2}) \rightarrow (\frac{14}{2}, \frac{-6}{2}) \rightarrow M(7, -3)$

Finding Distance of Two Points

✓ Use following formula to find the distance of two points with the coordinates A (x_1, y_1) and B (x_2, y_2):

$$d = \sqrt{(x_2 - x_1)^2 + (y_2 - y_1)^2}$$

Examples:

1) Find the distance between $(4, 6)$ *and* $(1, 2)$.

Solution: *Use distance of two points formula:* $d = \sqrt{(x_2 - x_1)^2 + (y_2 - y_1)^2}$

$(x_1, y_1) = (4, 6)$ and $(x_2, y_2) = (1, 2)$. *Then:* $d = \sqrt{(x_2 - x_1)^2 + (y_2 - y_1)^2} \rightarrow$

$$d = \sqrt{(1 - (4))^2 + (2 - 6)^2} = \sqrt{(-3)^2 + (-4)^2} = \sqrt{9 + 16} = \sqrt{25} = 5 \rightarrow d = 5$$

2) Find the distance of two points $(-6, -10)$ *and* $(-2, -10)$.

Solution: *Use distance of two points formula:* $d = \sqrt{(x_2 - x_1)^2 + (y_2 - y_1)^2}$

$(x_1, y_1) = (-6, -10)$, and $(x_2, y_2) = (-2, -10)$

Then: $d = \sqrt{(x_2 - x_1)^2 + (y_2 - y_1)^2} \rightarrow d = \sqrt{(-2 - (-6))^2 + (-10 - (-10))^2} =$

$\sqrt{(4)^2 + (0)^2} = \sqrt{16 + 0} = \sqrt{16} = 4$. Then: $d = 4$

3) Find the distance between $(-6, 5)$ *and* $(-2, 2)$.

Solution: *Use distance of two points formula:* $d = \sqrt{(x_2 - x_1)^2 + (y_2 - y_1)^2}$

$(x_1, y_1) = (-6, 5)$ and $(x_2, y_2) = (-2, 2)$. *Then:* $d = \sqrt{(x_2 - x_1)^2 + (y_2 - y_1)^2} \rightarrow$

$$d = \sqrt{(-2 - (-6))^2 + (2 - 5)^2} = \sqrt{(4)^2 + (-3)^2} = \sqrt{16 + 9} = \sqrt{25} = 5$$

Chapter 8: Practices

Find the slope of each line.

1) $y = x - 1$
2) $y = -2x + 5$
3) $y = 2x - 1$
4) *Line through* $(-2, 4)$ *and* $(6, 0)$
5) *Line through* $(-3, 5)$ *and* $(-2, 8)$
6) *Line through* $(-3, -1)$ *and* $(0, -4)$

Sketch the graph of each line. (Using Slope–Intercept Form)

7) $y = x + 2$

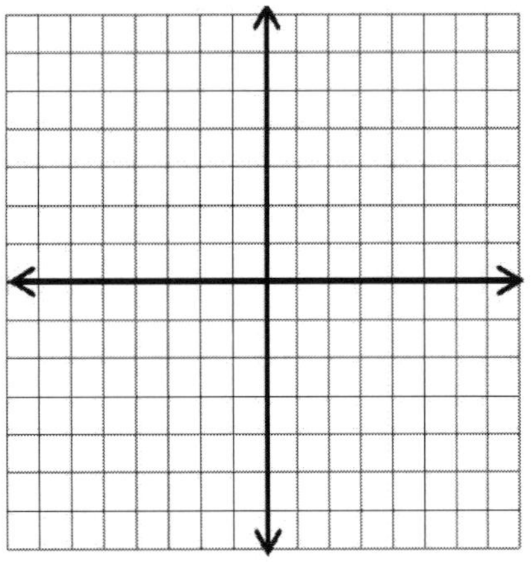

8) $y = 2x - 3$

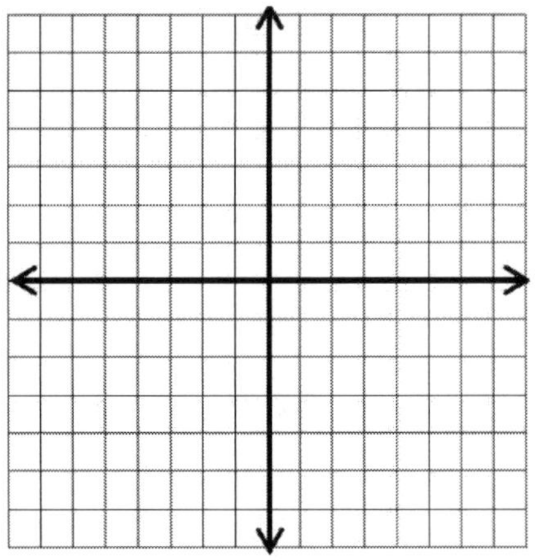

Solve.

9) What is the equation of a line with slope 4 and intercept 12? ________________

10) What is the equation of a line with slope 4 and passes through point $(4, 2)$?

____

11) What is the equation of a line with slope -2 and passes through point $(-2, 4)$?

____

12) The slope of a line is -3 and it passes through point $(-1, 5)$. What is the equation of the line? ________________

13) The slope of a line is 3 and it passes through point $(-1, 4)$. What is the equation of the line? ________________

Sketch the graph of each linear inequality. (Graphing Linear Inequalities)

15) $y > 3x - 1$

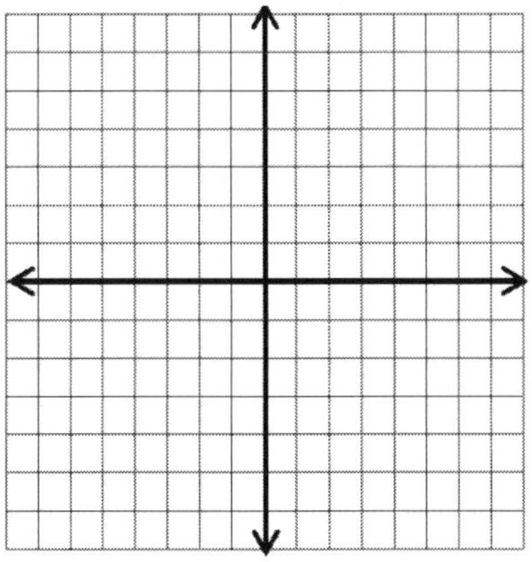

16) $y < -x + 4$

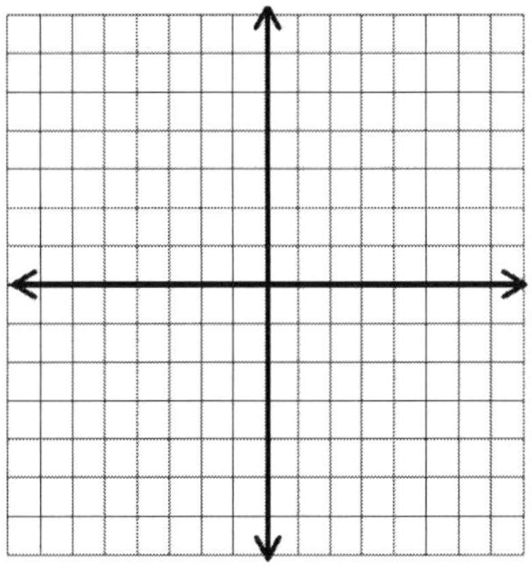

Find the midpoint of the line segment with the given endpoints.

17) $(2,5), (-2,7)$

18) $(-3,6), (5,2)$

19) $(9,-7), (-6,5)$

20) $(14,-8), (-4,-2)$

21) $(-11,2), (3,8)$

22) $(7,10), (1,-6)$

Find the distance between each pair of points.

23) $(3,10), (-2,-2)$

24) $(1,6), (4,10)$

25) $(-2,-1), (-8,7)$

26) $(8,-2), (5,-6)$

27) $(4,-3), (-5,9)$

28) $(0,6), (3,2)$

Answers – Chapter 8

Find the slope of the line through each pair of points.

1) 1
2) -2
3) 2
4) $-\frac{1}{2}$
5) 3
6) -1

Sketch the graph of each line. (Using Slope–Intercept Form)

7) $y = x + 2$

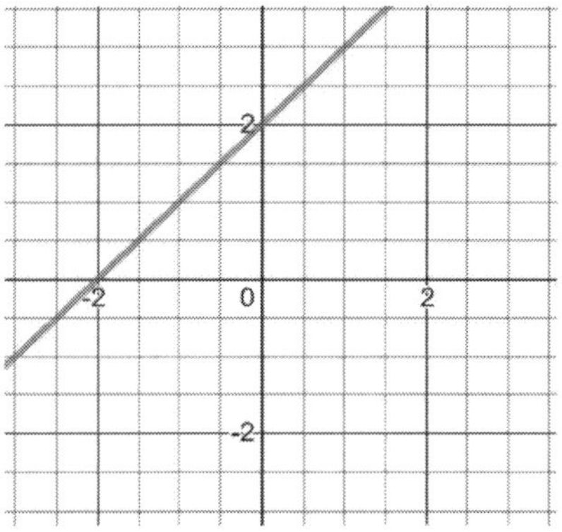

8) $y = 2x - 3$

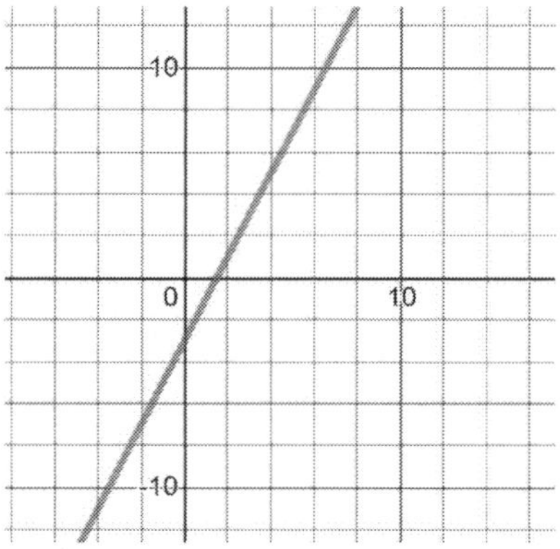

Write the equation of the line through the given points.

9) $y = 4x + 12$
10) $y = 4x - 14$
11) $y = -2x + 8$
12) $y = -3x + 2$
13) $y = 3x + 7$

Sketch the graph of each linear inequality. (Graphing Linear Inequalities)

15) $y > 3x - 1$

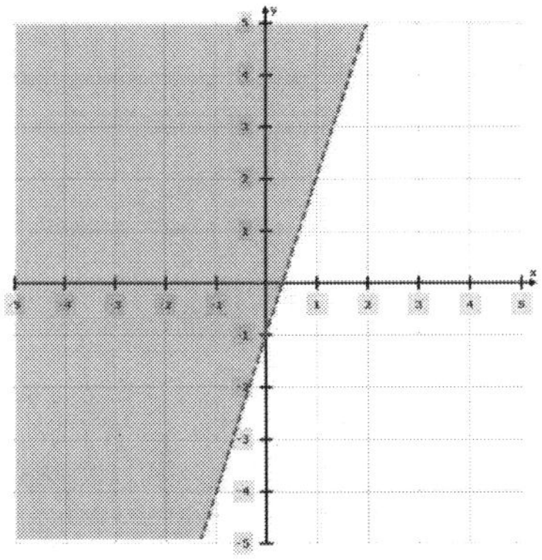

16) $y < -x + 4$

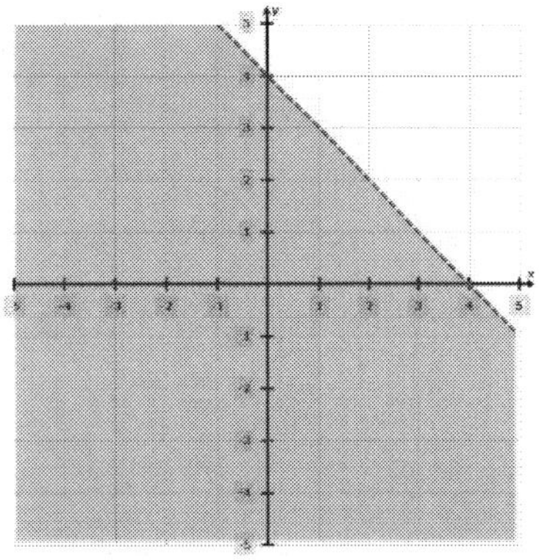

Find the midpoint of the line segment with the given endpoints.

17) $(0, 6)$
18) $(1, 4)$
19) $(1.5, -1)$
20) $(5, -5)$
21) $(-4, 5)$
22) $(4, 2)$

Find the distance between each pair of points.

23) 13
24) 5
25) 10
26) 5
27) 15
28) 5

Chapter 9:

Exponents and Variables

Math Topics that you'll learn in this Chapter:

- ✓ Multiplication Property of Exponents
- ✓ Division Property of Exponents
- ✓ Powers of Products and Quotients
- ✓ Zero and Negative Exponents
- ✓ Negative Exponents and Negative Bases
- ✓ Scientific Notation
- ✓ Radicals

Multiplication Property of Exponents

- Exponents are shorthand for repeated multiplication of the same number by itself. For example, instead of 2×2, we can write 2^2. For $3 \times 3 \times 3 \times 3$, we can write 3^4
- In algebra, a variable is a letter used to stand for a number. The most common letters are: $x, y, z, a, b, c, m,$ and n.
- Exponent's rules: $x^a \times x^b = x^{a+b}$, $\frac{x^a}{x^b} = x^{a-b}$

$(x^a)^b = x^{a \times b}$ $\qquad (xy)^a = x^a \times y^a$ $\qquad (\frac{a}{b})^c = \frac{a^c}{b^c}$

Examples:

1) *Multiply.* $4x^3 \times 2x^2$

Solution: Use Exponent's rules: $x^a \times x^b = x^{a+b} \rightarrow x^3 \times x^2 = x^{3+2} = x^5$

Then: $4x^3 \times 2x^2 = 8x^5$

2) *Simplify.* $(x^3y^5)^2$

Solution: Use Exponent's rules: $(x^a)^b = x^{a \times b}$. Then: $(x^3y^5)^2 = x^{3\times2}y^{5\times2} = x^6y^{10}$

3) *Multiply.* $-2x^5 \times 7x^3$

Solution: Use Exponent's rules: $x^a \times x^b = x^{a+b} \rightarrow x^5 \times x^3 = x^{5+3} = x^8$

Then: $-2x^5 \times 7x^3 = -14x^8$

4) *Simplify.* $(x^2y^4)^3$

Solution: Use Exponent's rules: $(x^a)^b = x^{a \times b}$. Then: $(x^2y^4)^3 = x^{2\times3}y^{4\times3} = x^6y^{12}$

Division Property of Exponents

- Exponents are shorthand for repeated multiplication of the same number by itself. For example, instead of 3×3, we can write 3^2. For $2 \times 2 \times 2$, we can write 2^3
- For division of exponents use following formulas:

$$\frac{x^a}{x^b} = x^{a-b}, x \neq 0, \qquad \frac{x^a}{x^b} = \frac{1}{x^{b-a}}, x \neq 0, \qquad \frac{1}{x^b} = x^{-b}$$

Examples:

1) *Simplify.* $\frac{12x^2y}{4xy^3} =$

Solution: First cancel the common factor: $4 \rightarrow \frac{12x^2y}{4xy^3} = \frac{3x^2y}{xy^3}$

Use Exponent's rules: $\frac{x^a}{x^b} = x^{a-b} \rightarrow \frac{x^2}{x} = x^{2-1} = x$ and $\frac{y}{y^3} = \frac{1}{y^{3-1}} = \frac{1}{y^2}$

Then: $\frac{12x^2y}{4xy^3} = \frac{3x}{y^2}$

2) *Simplify.* $\frac{18x^6}{2x^3} =$

Solution: Use Exponent's rules: $\frac{x^a}{x^b} = x^{b-a} \rightarrow \frac{x^6}{x^3} = x^{6-3} = x^3$

Then: $\frac{18x^6}{2x^3} = 9x^3$

3) *Simplify.* $\frac{8x^3y}{40x^2y^3} =$

Solution: First cancel the common factor: $8 \rightarrow \frac{8x^3y}{40x^2y^3} = \frac{x^3y}{5x^2y^3}$

Use Exponent's rules: $\frac{x^a}{x^b} = x^{a-b} \rightarrow \frac{x^3}{x^2} = x^{3-2} = x$

Then: $\frac{8x^3y}{40x^2y^3} = \frac{xy}{5y^3} \rightarrow$ now cancel the common factor: $y \rightarrow \frac{xy}{5y^3} = \frac{x}{5y^2}$

Powers of Products and Quotients

- Exponents are shorthand for repeated multiplication of the same number by itself. For example, instead of $2 \times 2 \times 2$, we can write 2^3. For $3 \times 3 \times 3 \times 3$, we can write 3^4
- For any nonzero numbers a and b and any integer x, $(ab)^x = a^x \times b^x$ and $(\frac{a}{b})^c = \frac{a^c}{b^c}$

Examples:

1) *Simplify.* $(6x^2y^4)^2$

Solution: Use Exponent's rules: $(x^a)^b = x^{a \times b}$

$(6x^2y^4)^2 = (6)^2(x^2)^2(y^4)^2 = 36x^{2\times2}y^{4\times2} = 36x^4y^8$

2) *Simplify.* $(\frac{5x}{2x^2})^2$

Solution: First cancel the common factor: $x \rightarrow (\frac{5x}{2x^2})^2 = (\frac{5}{2x})^2$

Use Exponent's rules: $(\frac{a}{b})^c = \frac{a^c}{b^c}$, Then: $(\frac{5}{2x})^2 = \frac{5^2}{(2x)^2} = \frac{25}{4x^2}$

3) *Simplify.* $(3x^5y^4)^2$

Solution: Use Exponent's rules: $(x^a)^b = x^{a \times b}$

$(3x^5y^4)^2 = (3)^2(x^5)^2(y^4)^2 = 9x^{5\times2}y^{4\times2} = 9x^{10}y^8$

4) *Simplify.* $(\frac{2x}{3x^2})^2$

Solution: First cancel the common factor: $x \rightarrow (\frac{2x}{3x^2})^2 = (\frac{2}{3x})^2$

Use Exponent's rules: $(\frac{a}{b})^c = \frac{a^c}{b^c}$, Then: $(\frac{2}{3x})^2 = \frac{2^2}{(3x)^2} = \frac{4}{9x^2}$

Zero and Negative Exponents

- Zero-Exponent Rule: $a^0 = 1$, this means that anything raised to the zero power is 1. For example: $(5xy)^0 = 1$
- A negative exponent simply means that the base is on the wrong side of the fraction line, so you need to flip the base to the other side. For instance, "x^{-2}" (pronounced as "ecks to the minus two") just means "x^2" but underneath, as in $\frac{1}{x^2}$.

Examples:

1) *Evaluate.* $(\frac{2}{3})^{-2} =$

Solution: Use negative exponent's rule: $\left(\frac{x^a}{x^b}\right)^{-2} = \left(\frac{x^b}{x^a}\right)^2 \rightarrow \left(\frac{2}{3}\right)^{-2} = \left(\frac{3}{2}\right)^2 =$

Then: $\left(\frac{3}{2}\right)^2 = \frac{3^2}{2^2} = \frac{9}{4}$

2) *Evaluate.* $(\frac{4}{5})^{-3} =$

Solution: Use negative exponent's rule: $\left(\frac{x^a}{x^b}\right)^{-2} = \left(\frac{x^b}{x^a}\right)^2 \rightarrow \left(\frac{4}{5}\right)^{-3} = \left(\frac{5}{4}\right)^3 =$

Then: $\left(\frac{5}{4}\right)^3 = \frac{5^3}{4^3} = \frac{125}{64}$

3) *Evaluate.* $(\frac{x}{y})^0 =$

Solution: Use zero-exponent Rule: $a^0 = 1$

Then: $(\frac{x}{y})^0 = 1$

4) *Evaluate.* $(\frac{5}{6})^{-1} =$

Solution: Use negative exponent's rule: $\left(\frac{x^a}{x^b}\right)^{-2} = \left(\frac{x^b}{x^a}\right)^2 \rightarrow \left(\frac{5}{6}\right)^{-1} = \left(\frac{6}{5}\right)^1 = \frac{6}{5}$

Negative Exponents and Negative Bases

- A negative exponent is the reciprocal of that number with a positive exponent. $(3)^{-2} = \frac{1}{3^2}$
- To simplify a negative exponent, make the power positive!
- The parenthesis is important! -5^{-2} is not the same as $(-5)^{-2}$

$$-5^{-2} = -\frac{1}{5^2} \text{ and } (-5)^{-2} = +\frac{1}{5^2}$$

Examples:

1) *Simplify.* $(\frac{5a}{6c})^{-2} =$

Solution: Use negative exponent's rule: $(\frac{x^a}{x^b})^{-2} = (\frac{x^b}{x^a})^2 \rightarrow (\frac{5a}{6c})^{-2} = (\frac{6c}{5a})^2$

Now use exponent's rule: $(\frac{a}{b})^c = \frac{a^c}{b^c} \rightarrow = (\frac{6c}{5a})^2 = \frac{6^2c^2}{5^2a^2}$

Then: $\frac{6^2c^2}{5^2a^2} = \frac{36c^2}{25a^2}$

2) *Simplify.* $(\frac{2x}{3yz})^{-3} =$

Solution: Use negative exponent's rule: $(\frac{x^a}{x^b})^{-2} = (\frac{x^b}{x^a})^2 \rightarrow (\frac{2x}{3yz})^{-3} = (\frac{3yz}{2x})^3$

Now use exponent's rule: $(\frac{a}{b})^c = \frac{a^c}{b^c} \rightarrow (\frac{3yz}{2x})^3 = \frac{3^3y^3z^3}{2^3x^3} = \frac{27y^3z^3}{8x^3}$

3) *Simplify.* $(\frac{3a}{2c})^{-2} =$

Solution: Use negative exponent's rule: $(\frac{x^a}{x^b})^{-2} = (\frac{x^b}{x^a})^2 \rightarrow (\frac{3a}{2c})^{-2} = (\frac{2c}{3a})^2$

Now use exponent's rule: $(\frac{a}{b})^c = \frac{a^c}{b^c} \rightarrow = (\frac{2c}{3a})^2 = \frac{2^2c^2}{3^2a^2}$

Then: $\frac{2^2c^2}{3^2a^2} = \frac{4c^2}{9a^2}$

Scientific Notation

- Scientific notation is used to write very big or very small numbers in decimal form.
- In scientific notation all numbers are written in the form of: $m \times 10^n$, where m is greater than 1 and less than 10.
- To convert a number from scientific notation to standard form, move the decimal point to the left (if the exponent of ten is a negative number), or to the right (if the exponent is positive).

Examples:

1) *Write* 0.00015 *in scientific notation.*

Solution: First, move the decimal point to the right so that you have a number that is between 1 and 10. That number is 1.5

Now, determine how many places the decimal moved in step 1 by the power of 10. We moved the decimal point 4 digits to the right. Then: 10^{-4} → When the decimal moved to the right, the exponent is negative. Then: $0.00015 = 1.5 \times 10^{-4}$

2) *Write* $\mathbf{9.5 \times 10^{-5}}$ *in standard notation.*

Solution: 10^{-5} → When the decimal moved to the right, the exponent is negative.

Then: $9.5 \times 10^{-5} = 0.000095$

3) *Write* $\mathbf{0.00012}$ *in scientific notation.*

Solution: First, move the decimal point to the right so that you have a number that is between 1 and 10. Then: $m = 1.2$

Now, determine how many places the decimal moved in step 1 by the power of 10.

10^{-4} → Then: $0.00012 = 1.2 \times 10^{-4}$

4) *Write* $\mathbf{8.3 \times 10^{5}}$ *in standard notation.*

Solution: 10^{-5} → The exponent is positive 5. Then, move the decimal point to the right five digits. (remember $8.3 = 8.30000$)

Then: $8.3 \times 10^5 = 830000$

Radicals

- If n is a positive integer and x is a real number, then: $\sqrt[n]{x} = x^{\frac{1}{n}}$, $\sqrt[n]{xy} = x^{\frac{1}{n}} \times y^{\frac{1}{n}}$, $\sqrt[n]{\frac{x}{y}} = \frac{x^{\frac{1}{n}}}{y^{\frac{1}{n}}}$, and $\sqrt[n]{x} \times \sqrt[n]{y} = \sqrt[n]{xy}$
- A square root of x is a number r whose square is: $r^2 = x$ (r is a square root of x.
- To add and subtract radicals, we need to have the same values under the radical. For example: $\sqrt{3} + \sqrt{3} = 2\sqrt{3}$, $3\sqrt{5} - \sqrt{5} = 2\sqrt{5}$

Examples:

1) *Find the square root of* $\sqrt{169}$.

Solution: First factor the number: $169 = 13^2$,

Then: $\sqrt{169} = \sqrt{13^2}$

Now use radical rule: $\sqrt[n]{a^n} = a$.

Then: $\sqrt{169} = \sqrt{13^2} = 13$

2) *Evaluate.* $\sqrt{9} \times \sqrt{25} =$

Solution: Find the values of $\sqrt{9}$ and $\sqrt{25}$.

Then: $\sqrt{9} \times \sqrt{25} = 3 \times 5 = 15$

3) *Solve.* $7\sqrt{2} + 4\sqrt{2}$.

Solution: Since we have the same values under the radical, we can add these two radicals: $7\sqrt{2} + 4\sqrt{2} = 11\sqrt{2}$

4) *Evaluate.* $\sqrt{2} \times \sqrt{8} =$

Solution: Use this radical rule: $\sqrt[n]{x} \times \sqrt[n]{y} = \sqrt[n]{xy} \rightarrow \sqrt{2} \times \sqrt{8} = \sqrt{16}$

The square root of 16 is 4. Then: $\sqrt{2} \times \sqrt{8} = \sqrt{16} = 4$

Chapter 9: Practices

Simplify and write the answer in exponential form.

1) $3x^3 \times 5xy^2 =$

2) $4x^2y \times 6x^2y^2 =$

3) $8x^3y^2 \times 2x^2y^3 =$

4) $7xy^4 \times 3x^2y =$

5) $6x^4y^5 \times 8x^3y^2 =$

6) $5x^3y^3 \times 8x^3y^3 =$

Simplify. (Division Property of Exponents)

7) $\frac{5^5 \times 5^3}{5^9 \times 5} =$

8) $\frac{8x}{24x^2} =$

9) $\frac{15\ \ ^4}{9x^3} =$

10) $\frac{36\ \ ^3}{54\ \ ^3y^2} =$

11) $\frac{14y^3}{49x^4y^4} =$

12) $\frac{120x^3y^5}{30\ \ ^2y^3} =$

Simplify. (Powers of Products and Quotients)

13) $(8x^4y^6)^3 =$

14) $(3x^5y^4)^6 =$

15) $(5x \times 4xy^2)^2 =$

16) $(\frac{6x}{x^3})^2 =$

17) $\left(\frac{2x^3y^5}{6x^4y^2}\right)^2 =$

18) $\left(\frac{42x^4y^6}{21\ \ ^3y^5}\right)^3 =$

Evaluate the following expressions. (Zero and Negative Exponents)

19) $(\frac{2}{5})^{-2} =$

20) $(\frac{1}{2})^{-8} =$

21) $(\frac{2}{5})^{-3} =$

22) $(\frac{3}{7})^{-2} =$

23) $(\frac{5}{6})^{-3} =$

24) $(\frac{4}{9})^{-2} =$

Simplify. (Negative Exponents and Negative Bases)

25) $16x^{-3}y^{-4} =$

26) $-9x^2y^{-3} =$

27) $12a^{-4}b^2 =$

28) $25a^3b^{-5}c^{-1} =$

29) $\frac{18y}{x^2y^{-2}} =$

30) $\frac{21a^{-2}b}{-14c^{-4}} =$

Write each number in scientific notation.

31) $0.00615 =$

32) $0.000048 =$

33) $36{,}000 =$

34) $82{,}000{,}000 =$

Evaluate.

35) $\sqrt{7} \times \sqrt{7} =$ ________

36) $\sqrt{36} - \sqrt{9} =$ ________

37) $\sqrt{25} + \sqrt{49} =$ ________

38) $\sqrt{16} \times \sqrt{64} =$ ________

39) $\sqrt{3} \times \sqrt{12} =$ ________

40) $2\sqrt{6} + 3\sqrt{6} =$ ________

Answers – Chapter 9

1) $15x^4y^2$
2) $24x^4y^3$
3) $16x^5y^5$
4) $21x^3y^5$
5) $48x^7y^7$
6) $40x^6y^6$
7) $\frac{1}{25}$
8) $\frac{1}{3x}$
9) $\frac{5}{3}x$
10) $\frac{2}{3y^3}$
11) $\frac{2}{7x^4y}$
12) $4xy^2$
13) $512x^{12}y^{18}$
14) $729x^{30}y^{24}$
15) $400x^4y^4$
16) $\frac{36}{x^4}$
17) $\frac{y^6}{9x^2}$
18) $8x^3y^3$
19) $\frac{25}{4}$
20) 256
21) $\frac{125}{8}$
22) $\frac{49}{9}$
23) $\frac{216}{125}$
24) $\frac{81}{16}$
25) $\frac{16}{x^3\,y^4}$
26) $-\frac{9x^2}{y^3}$
27) $\frac{12b^2}{a^4}$
28) $\frac{25a^3}{b^5c}$
29) $\frac{18y^3}{x^2}$
30) $-\frac{3bc^4}{2a^2}$
31) 6.15×10^{-3}
32) 4.8×10^{-5}
33) 3.6×10^4
34) 8.2×10^7
35) 7
36) 3
37) 12
38) 32
39) 6
40) $5\sqrt{6}$

Chapter 10:

Polynomials

Math Topics that you'll learn in this Chapter:

- ✓ Simplifying Polynomials
- ✓ Adding and Subtracting Polynomials
- ✓ Multiplying Monomials
- ✓ Multiplying and Dividing Monomials
- ✓ Multiplying a Polynomial and a Monomial
- ✓ Multiplying Binomials
- ✓ Factoring Trinomials

Simplifying Polynomials

- To simplify Polynomials, find "like" terms. (they have same variables with same power).
- Use "FOIL". (First-Out-In-Last) for binomials:

$$(x+a)(x+b) = x^2 + (b+a)x + ab$$

- Add or Subtract "like" terms using order of operation.

Examples:

1) Simplify this expression. $x(2x+5)+6x =$

Solution: Use Distributive Property: $x(2x+5) = 2x^2 + 5x$

Now, combine like terms: $x(2x+5)+6x = 2x^2 + 5x + 6x = 2x^2 + 11x$

2) Simplify this expression. $(x+2)(x+3) =$

Solution: First apply FOIL method: $(a+b)(c+d) = ac + ad + bc + bd$

$(x+2)(x+3) = x^2 + 3x + 2x + 6$

Now combine like terms: $x^2 + 3x + 2x + 6 \; = x^2 + 5x + 6$

3) Simplify this expression. $4x(2x-3) + 6x^2 - 4x =$

Solution: Use Distributive Property: $4x(2x-3) = 8x^2 - 12x$

Then: $4x(2x-3) + 6x^2 - 4x = 8x^2 - 12x + 6x^2 - 4x$

Now combine like terms: $8x^2 + 6x^2 = 14x^2$, and $-12x - 4x = -16x$

The simplified form of the expression: $8x^2 - 12x + 6x^2 - 4x = 14x^2 - 16x$

Adding and Subtracting Polynomials

- Adding polynomials is just a matter of combining like terms, with some order of operations considerations thrown in.
- Be careful with the minus signs, and don't confuse addition and multiplication!
- For subtracting polynomials, sometimes you need to use the Distributive Property: $a(b+c) = ab + ac$, $a(b-c) = ab - ac$

Examples:

1) *Simplify the expressions.* $(x^3 - 3x^4) - (2x^4 - 5x^3) =$

Solution: First use Distributive Property: $-(2x^4 - 5x^3) = -1(2x^4 - 5x^3) = -2x^4 + 5x^3$

$\rightarrow (x^3 - 3x^4) - (2x^4 - 5x^3) = x^3 - 3x^4 - 2x^4 + 5x^3$

Now combine like terms: $x^3 + 5x^3 = 6x^3$ and $-3x^4 - 2x^4 = -5x^4$

Then: $(x^3 - 3x^4) - (2x^4 - 5x^3) = x^3 - 3x^4 - 2x^4 + 5x^3 = 6x^3 - 5x^4$

Write the answer in standard form: $6x^3 - 5x^4 = -5x^4 + 6x^3$

2) *Add expressions.* $(2x^3 - 4) + (6x^3 - 2x^2) =$

Solution: Remove parentheses: $(2x^3 - 4) + (6x^3 - 2x^2) = 2x^3 - 4 + 6x^3 - 2x^2$

Now combine like terms: $2x^3 - 4 + 6x^3 - 2x^2 = 8x^3 - 2x^2 - 4$

3) *Simplify the expressions.* $(8x^2 - 3x^3) - (2x^2 + 5x^3) =$

Solution: First use Distributive Property: $-(2x^2 + 5x^3) = -2x^2 - 5x^3 \rightarrow$

$(8x^2 - 3x^3) - (2x^2 + 5x^3) = 8x^2 - 3x^3 - 2x^2 - 5x^3$

Now combine like terms and write in standard form: $8x^2 - 3x^3 - 2x^2 - 5x^3 = -8x^3 + 6x^2$

Multiplying Monomials

- A monomial is a polynomial with just one term: Examples: $2x$ or $7y^2$.
- When you multiply monomials, first multiply the coefficients (a number placed before and multiplying the variable) and then multiply the variables using multiplication property of exponents.

$$x^a \times x^b = x^{a+b}$$

Examples:

1) *Multiply expressions.* $5xy^4z^2 \times 3x^2y^5z^3$

Solution: Find same variables and use multiplication property of exponents: $x^a \times x^b = x^{a+b}$

$x \times x^2 = x^{1+2} = x^3$, $y^4 \times y^5 = y^{4+5} = y^9$ and $z^2 \times z^3 = z^{2+3} = z^5$

Then, multiply coefficients and variables: $5xy^4z^2 \times 3x^2y^5z^3 = 15x^3y^9z^5$

2) *Multiply expressions.* $-2a^5b^4 \times 8a^3b^4 =$

Solution: Use multiplication property of exponents: $x^a \times x^b = x^{a+b}$

$a^5 \times a^3 = a^{5+3} = a^8$ and $b^4 \times b^4 = b^{4+4} = b^8$

Then: $-2a^5b^4 \times 8a^3b^4 = -16a^8b^8$

3) *Multiply.* $7xy^3z^5 \times 4x^2y^4z^3$

Solution: Use multiplication property of exponents: $x^a \times x^b = x^{a+b}$

$x \times x^2 = x^{1+2} = x^3$, $y^3 \times y^4 = y^{3+4} = y^7$ and $z^5 \times z^3 = z^{5+3} = z^8$

Then: $7xy^3z^5 \times 4x^2y^5z^3 = 28x^3y^7z^8$

4) *Simplify.* $(5a^6b^3)(-9a^7b^2) =$

Solution: Use multiplication property of exponents: $x^a \times x^b = x^{a+b}$

$a^6 \times a^7 = a^{6+7} = a^{13}$ and $b^3 \times b^2 = b^{3+2} = b^5$

Then: $(5a^6b^3) \times (-9a^6b^2) = -45a^{13}b^5$

Multiplying and Dividing Monomials

- When you divide or multiply two monomials you need to divide or multiply their coefficients and then divide or multiply their variables.
- In case of exponents with the same base, for Division, subtract their powers, for Multiplication, add their powers.
- Exponent's Multiplication and Division rules:

$$x^a \times x^b = x^{a+b}, \qquad \frac{x^a}{x^b} = x^{a-b}$$

Examples:

1) *Multiply expressions.* $(-5x^8)(4x^6) =$

Solution: Use multiplication property of exponents: $x^a \times x^b = x^{a+b} \rightarrow x^8 \times x^6 = x^{14}$

Then: $(-5x^5)(4x^4) = -20x^{14}$

2) *Divide expressions.* $\frac{14x^5y^4}{2xy^3} =$

Solution: Use division property of exponents: $\frac{x^a}{x^b} = x^{a-b} \rightarrow \frac{x^5}{x} = x^{5-1} = x^4$ and $\frac{y^4}{y^3} = y$

Then: $\frac{14x^5y^4}{2xy^3} = 7x^4y$

3) *Divide expressions.* $\frac{56a^8b^3}{8ab^3}$

Solution: Use division property of exponents: $\frac{x^a}{x^b} = x^{a-b} \rightarrow \frac{a^8}{a} = a^{8-1} = a^7$ and $\frac{b^3}{b^3} = 1$

Then: $\frac{56a^8b^3}{8ab^3} = 7a^7$

Multiplying a Polynomial and a Monomial

- When multiplying monomials, use the product rule for exponents.

$$x^a \times x^b = x^{a+b}$$

- When multiplying a monomial by a polynomial, use the distributive property.

$$a \times (b + c) = a \times b + a \times c = ab + ac$$
$$a \times (b - c) = a \times b - a \times c = ab - ac$$

Examples:

1) *Multiply expressions.* $5x(3x - 2)$

Solution: Use Distributive Property: $5x(3x - 2) = 5x \times 3x - 5x \times (-2) = 15x^2 - 10x$

2) *Multiply expressions.* $x(2x^2 + 3y^2)$

Solution: Use Distributive Property: $x(2x^2 + 3y^2) = x \times 2x^2 + x \times 3y^2 = 2x^3 + 3xy^2$

3) *Multiply.* $-4x(-5x^2 + 3x - 6)$

Solution: Use Distributive Property:

$-4x(-5x^2 + 3x - 6) = (-4x)(-5x^2) + (-4x) \times (3x) + (-4x) \times (-6) =$

Now, simplify: $(-4x)(-5x^2) + (-4x) \times (3x) + (-4x) \times (-6) = 20x^3 - 12x^2 + 24x$

Multiplying Binomials

- ✓ A binomial is a polynomial that is the sum or the difference of two terms, each of which is a monomial.
- ✓ To multiply two binomials, use "FOIL" method. (First-Out-In-Last)

$$(x+a)(x+b) = x \times x + x \times b + a \times x + a \times b = x^2 + bx + ax + ab$$

Examples:

1) *Multiply Binomials.* $(x+2)(x-4) =$

Solution: Use "FOIL". (First–Out–In–Last): $(x+2)(x-4) = x^2 - 4x + 2x - 8$

Then combine like terms: $x^2 - 4x + 2x - 8 = x^2 - 2x - 8$

2) *Multiply.* $(x-5)(x-2) =$

Solution: Use "FOIL". (First–Out–In–Last): $(x-5)(x-2) = x^2 - 2x - 5x + 10$

Then simplify: $x^2 - 2x - 5x + 10 = x^2 - 7x + 10$

3) *Multiply.* $(x-3)(x+6) =$

Solution: Use "FOIL". (First–Out–In–Last): $(x-3)(x+6) = x^2 + 6x - 3x - 18$

Then simplify: $x^2 + 6x - 3x - 18 = x^2 + 3x - 18$

4) *Multiply Binomials.* $(x+8)(x+4) =$

Solution: Use "FOIL". (First–Out–In–Last): $(x+8)(x+4) = x^2 + 4x + 8x + 32$

Then combine like terms: $x^2 + 4x + 8x + 32 = x^2 + 12x + 32$

Factoring Trinomials

To factor trinomials, you can use following methods:

- ✓ "FOIL": $(x + a)(x + b) = x^2 + (b + a)x + ab$
- ✓ "Difference of Squares":

$$a^2 - b^2 = (a + b)(a - b)$$

$$a^2 + 2ab + b^2 = (a + b)(a + b)$$

$$a^2 - 2ab + b^2 = (a - b)(a - b)$$

- ✓ "Reverse FOIL": $x^2 + (b + a)x + ab = (x + a)(x + b)$

Examples:

1) ***Factor this trinomial.*** $x^2 - 2x - 8$

Solution: Break the expression into groups. You need to find two numbers that their product is -8 and their sum is -2. (remember "Reverse FOIL": $x^2 + (b + a)x + ab = (x + a)(x + b)$). Those two numbers are 2 and -4. Then:

$x^2 - 2x - 8 = (x^2 + 2x) + (-4x - 8)$

Now factor out x from $x^2 + 2x : x(x + 2)$, and factor out -4 from $-4x - 8$: $-4(x + 2)$

Then: $(x^2 + 2x) + (-4x - 8) = x(x + 2) - 4(x + 2)$

Now factor out like term: $(x + 2)$. Then: $(x + 2)(x - 4)$

2) ***Factor this trinomial.*** $x^2 - 2x - 24$

Solution: Break the expression into groups: $(x^2 + 4x) + (-6x - 24)$

Now factor out x from $x^2 + 4x : x(x + 4)$, and factor out -6 from $-6x - 24$: $-6(x + 4)$

Then: $(x + 4) - 6(x + 4)$, now factor out like term:

$(x = 4) \rightarrow x(x + 4) - 6(x + 4) = (x + 4)(x - 6)$

Chapter 10: Practices

Simplify each polynomial.

1) $4(3x+5) =$
2) $8(6x-1) =$
3) $2x(7x+4)+2x =$
4) $5x(6x+2)-4x =$
5) $7x(3x-6)+x^2-2 =$
6) $3x^2-5-9x(4x+1) =$

Add or subtract polynomials.

7) $(6x^2+8)+(2x^2-4) =$
8) $(x^2-5x)-(3x^2+2x) =$
9) $(9x^3-4x^2)+(x^3-3x^2) =$
10) $(7x^3-3x)-(6x^3-5x) =$
11) $(12x^3+x^2)+(2x^2-10) =$
12) $(4x^3-15)-(3x^3-7x^2) =$

Simplify each expression. (Multiplying Monomials)

13) $5x^3 \times 6x^4 =$
14) $-4a^2b \times 3ab^2 =$
15) $(-7x^2yz) \times (-3xy^3z^2) =$
16) $9u^4t^2 \times (-4ut) =$
17) $12x^3z \times 3xy^2 =$
18) $-8a^2bc \times a^3b^2 =$

Simplify each expression. (Multiplying and Dividing Monomials)

19) $(4x^3y^4)(12x^5y^2) =$
20) $(5x^4y^2)(8x^6y^5) =$
21) $(16x^7y^9)(3x^6y^4) =$
22) $\frac{36x^5y^3}{9x^2y} =$
23) $\frac{98x^{12}y^{10}}{7x^9y^7} =$
24) $\frac{225x^9y^{13}}{15x^6y^9} =$

Find each product. (Multiplying a Polynomial and a Monomial)

25) $4x(6x - y) =$

26) $7x(3x + 5y) =$

27) $5x(x - 8y) =$

28) $x(3x^2 + 2x - 6) =$

29) $5x(-x^2 + 7x + 4) =$

30) $6x(6x^2 - 3x - 12) =$

Find each product. (Multiplying Binomials)

31) $(x - 3)(x + 3) =$

32) $(x - 5)(x - 4) =$

33) $(x + 6)(x + 3) =$

34) $(x - 7)(x + 8) =$

35) $(x + 2)(x - 9) =$

36) $(x - 15)(x + 3) =$

Factor each trinomial.

37) $x^2 + 4x - 12 =$

38) $x^2 + x - 20 =$

39) $x^2 + 3x - 108 =$

40) $x^2 + 12x + 32 =$

41) $x^2 - 14x + 48 =$

42) $x^2 + 2x - 35 =$

Answers – Chapter 10

1) $12x + 20$
2) $48x - 8$
3) $14x^2 + 10x$
4) $30x^2 + 6x$
5) $22x^2 - 42x - 2$
6) $-33x^2 - 9x - 5$

7) $8x^2 + 4$
8) $-2x^2 - 7x$
9) $10x^3 - 7x^2$
10) $x^3 + 2x$
11) $12x^3 + 3x^2 - 10$
12) $x^3 + 7x^2 - 15$

13) $30x^7$
14) $-12a^3b^3$
15) $21x^3y^4z^3$
16) $-36u^5t^3$
17) $36x^4y^2z$
18) $-8a^5b^3c$

19) $48x^8y^6$
20) $40x^{10}y^7$
21) $48x^{13}y^{13}$
22) $4x^3y^2$
23) $14x^3y^3$
24) $15x^3y^4$

25) $24x^2 - 4xy$
26) $21x^2 + 35xy$
27) $5x^2 - 40xy$
28) $3x^3 + 2x^2 - 6x$
29) $-5x^3 + 35x^2 + 20x$
30) $36x^3 - 18x^2 - 72x$

31) $x^2 - 9$
32) $x^2 - 9x + 20$
33) $x^2 + 9x + 18$
34) $x^2 + x - 56$
35) $x^2 - 7x - 18$
36) $x^2 - 12x - 45$

37) $(x - 2)(x + 6)$
38) $(x + 5)(x - 4)$
39) $(x + 12)(x - 9)$
40) $(x + 8)(x + 4)$
41) $(x - 6)(x - 8)$
42) $(x + 7)(x - 5)$

Chapter 11:

Geometry and Solid Figures

Math Topics that you'll learn in this Chapter:

- ✓ The Pythagorean Theorem
- ✓ Triangles
- ✓ Polygons
- ✓ Circles
- ✓ Trapezoids
- ✓ Cubes
- ✓ Rectangle Prisms
- ✓ Cylinder

The Pythagorean Theorem

- You can use the Pythagorean Theorem to find a missing side in a right triangle.
- In any right triangle: $a^2 + b^2 = c^2$

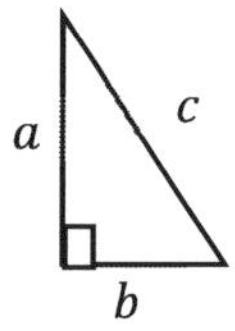

Examples:

1) Right triangle ABC (not shown) has two legs of lengths 6 cm (AB) and 8 cm (AC). What is the length of the hypotenuse of the triangle (side BC)?

Solution: Use Pythagorean Theorem: $a^2 + b^2 = c^2$, $a = 6$, and $b = 8$

Then: $a^2 + b^2 = c^2 \rightarrow 6^2 + 8^2 = c^2 \rightarrow 36 + 64 = c^2 \rightarrow 100 = c^2 \rightarrow c = \sqrt{100} = 10$

The length of the hypotenuse is 10 cm.

2) Find the hypotenuse of the following triangle.

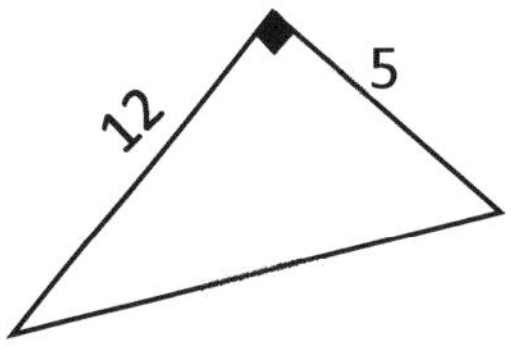

Solution: Use Pythagorean Theorem: $a^2 + b^2 = c^2$

Then: $a^2 + b^2 = c^2 \rightarrow 12^2 + 5^2 = c^2 \rightarrow 144 + 25 = c^2$

$c^2 = 169 \rightarrow c = \sqrt{169} = 13$

3) Find the length of the missing side in the following triangle.

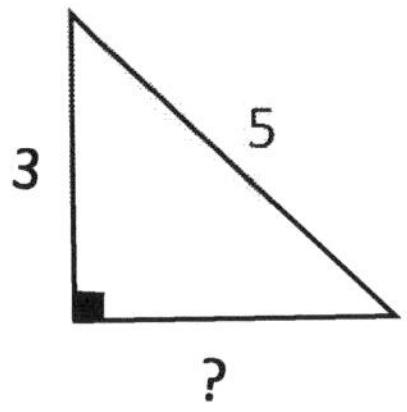

Solution: Use Pythagorean Theorem: $a^2 + b^2 = c^2$

Then: $a^2 + b^2 = c^2 \rightarrow 3^2 + b^2 = 5^2 \rightarrow 9 + b^2 = 25 \rightarrow$

$b^2 = 25 - 9 \rightarrow b^2 = 16 \rightarrow b = \sqrt{16} = 4$

Triangles

- In any triangle the sum of all angles is 180 degrees.
- Area of a triangle $= \frac{1}{2}\ (base \times height)$

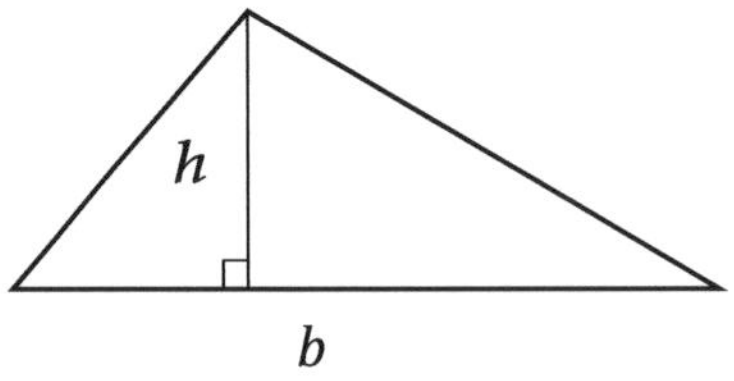

Examples:

What is the area of following triangles?

1)

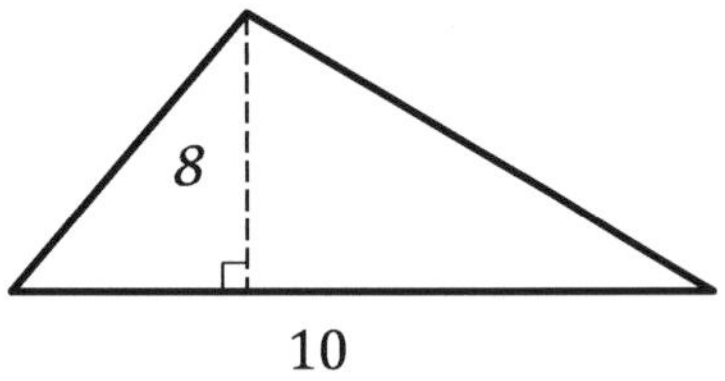

Solution:

Use the area formula: Area $= \frac{1}{2}\ (base\ \times height)$

$base = 10$ and $height = 8$

Area $= \frac{1}{2}(10 \times 8) = \frac{1}{2}(80) = 40$

2)

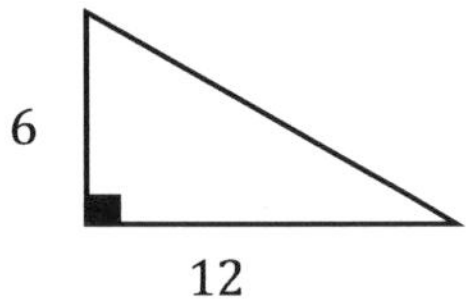

Solution:

Use the area formula: Area $= \frac{1}{2}\ (base \times height)$

$base = 12$ and $height = 6$

Area $= \frac{1}{2}(12 \times 6) = \frac{72}{2} = 36$

3) What is the missing angle in the following triangle?

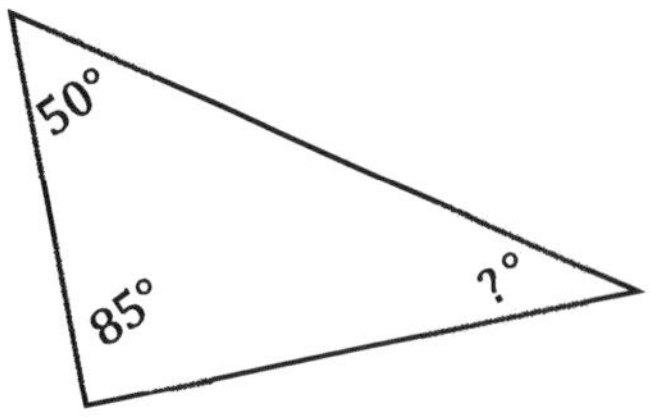

Solution:

In any triangle the sum of all angles is 180 degrees.

Let x be the missing angle. Then: $50 + 85 + x = 180$

$\rightarrow 135 + x = 180 \rightarrow x = 180 - 135 = 45$

The missing angle is 45 degrees.

Polygons

✅ Perimeter of a square

$= 4 \times side = 4s$

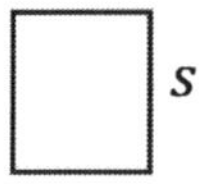

✅ Perimeter of a rectangle

$= 2(width + length)$

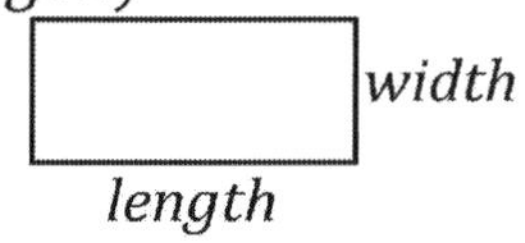

✅ Perimeter of trapezoid

$= a + b + c + d$

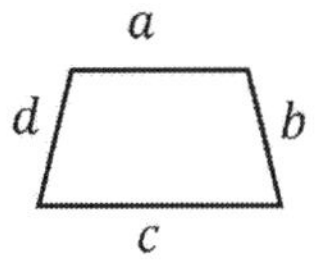

✅ Perimeter of a regular hexagon $= 6a$

✅ Perimeter of a parallelogram $= 2(l + w)$

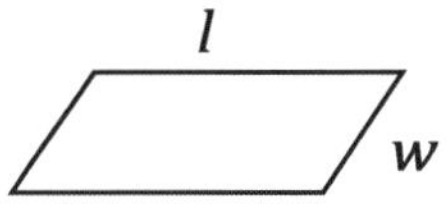

Examples:

1) Find the perimeter of following regular hexagon.

Solution: Since the hexagon is regular, all sides are equal.

Then: Perimeter of Hexagon $= 6 \times (one\ side)$

Perimeter of Hexagon $= 6 \times (one\ side) = 6 \times 4 = 24\ m$

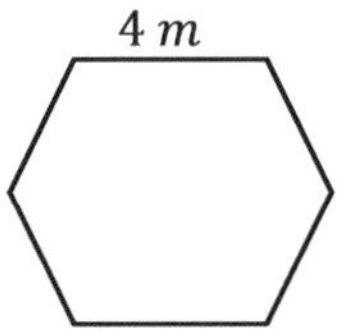

2) Find the perimeter of following trapezoid.

Solution: Perimeter of a trapezoid $= a + b + c + d$

Perimeter of the trapezoid $= 5 + 6 + 6 + 8 = 25\ ft$

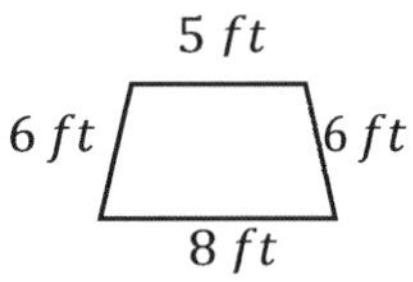

Circles

- In a circle, variable r is usually used for the radius and d for diameter.
- $Area\ of\ a\ circle = \pi r^2$ (π is about 3.14)
- $Circumference\ of\ a\ circle = 2\pi r$

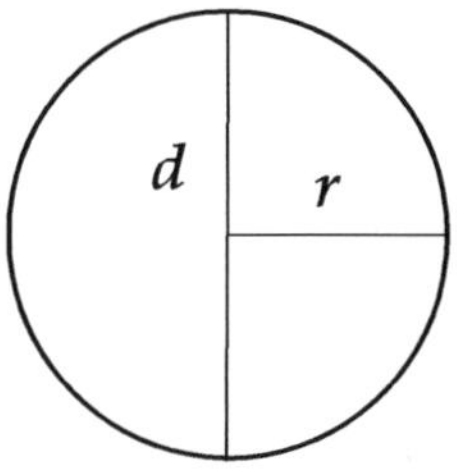

Examples:

1) Find the area of the following circle.

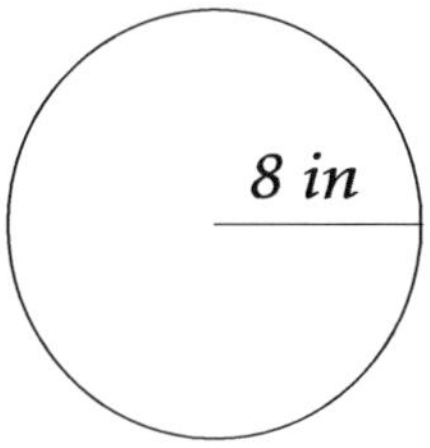

Solution:

Use area formula: $Area = \pi r^2$

$r = 8\ in \rightarrow Area = \pi(8)^2 = 64\pi, \pi = 3.14$

Then: $Area = 64 \times 3.14 = 200.96\ in^2$

2) Find the Circumference of the following circle.

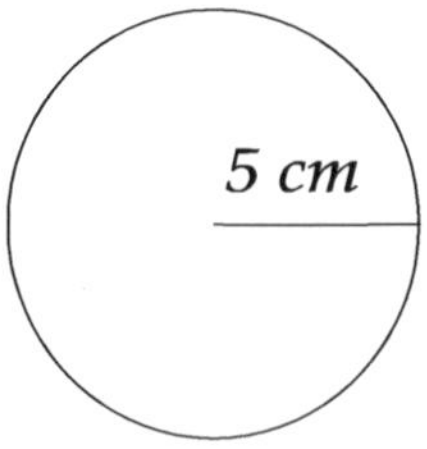

Solution:

Use Circumference formula: $Circumference = 2\pi r$

$r = 5\ cm \rightarrow Circumference = 2\pi(5) = 10\pi$

$\pi = 3.14$ ***Then:*** $Circumference = 10 \times 3.14 = 31.4\ cm$

3) Find the area of the circle.

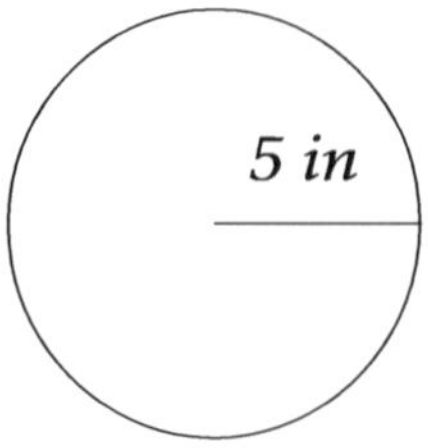

Solution:

Use area formula: $Area = \pi r^2$,

$r = 5\ in$ then: $Area = \pi(5)^2 = 25\pi, \pi = 3.14$

Then: $Area = 25 \times 3.14 = 78.5$

Trapezoids

- A quadrilateral with at least one pair of parallel sides is a trapezoid.
- Area of a trapezoid $= \frac{1}{2}h(b_1 + b_2)$

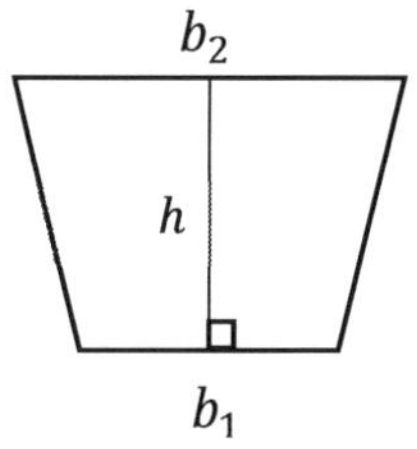

Examples:

1) Calculate the area of the following trapezoid.

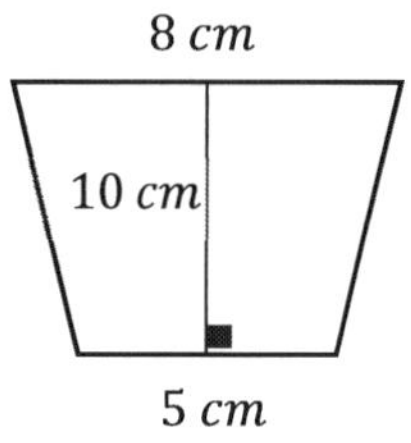

Solution:

Use area formula: $A = \frac{1}{2}h(b_1 + b_2)$

$b_1 = 5\ cm$, $b_2 = 8\ cm$ and $h = 10\ cm$

Then: $A = \frac{1}{2}(10)(8 + 5) = 5(13) = 65\ cm^2$

2) Calculate the area of the following trapezoid.

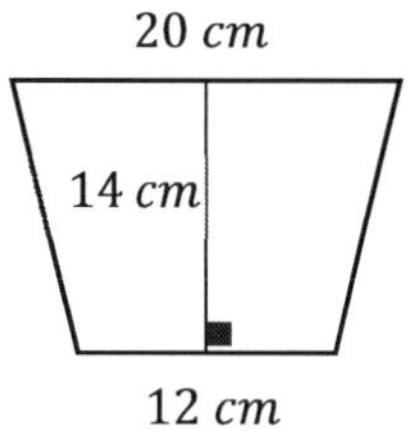

Solution:

Use area formula: $A = \frac{1}{2}h(b_1 + b_2)$

$b_1 = 12\ cm$, $b_2 = 20\ cm$ and $h = 14\ cm$

Then: $A = \frac{1}{2}(14)(12 + 20) = 7(32) = 224\ cm^2$

Cubes

- A cube is a three-dimensional solid object bounded by six square sides.
- Volume is the measure of the amount of space inside of a solid figure, like a cube, ball, cylinder or pyramid.
- Volume of a cube $= (\boldsymbol{one\ side})^3$
- surface area of a cube $= \mathbf{6} \times (\boldsymbol{one\ side})^2$

Examples:

1) Find the volume and surface area of the following cube.

Solution: Use volume formula: $volume = (one\ side)^3$

Then: $volume = (one\ side)^3 = (2)^3 = 8\ cm^3$

Use surface area formula: $surface\ area\ of\ cube: 6(one\ side)^2 = 6(2)^2 = 6(4) = 24\ cm^2$

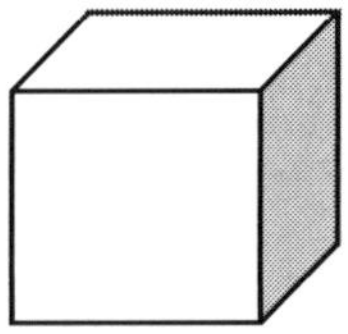

2) Find the volume and surface area of the following cube.

Solution: Use volume formula: $volume = (one\ side)^3$

Then: $volume = (one\ side)^3 = (5)^3 = 125\ cm^3$

Use surface area formula:

$surface\ area\ of\ cube: 6(one\ side)^2 = 6(5)^2 = 6(25) = 150\ cm^2$

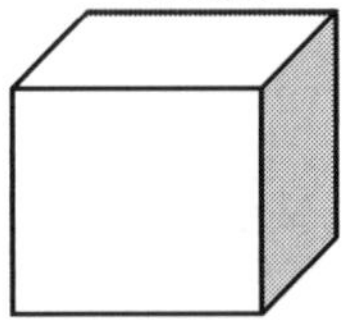

3) Find the volume and surface area of the following cube.

Solution: Use volume formula: $volume = (one\ side)^3$

Then: $volume = (one\ side)^3 = (7)^3 = 343\ m^3$

Use surface area formula:

$surface\ area\ of\ cube: 6(one\ side)^2 = 6(7)^2 = 6(49) = 294\ m^2$

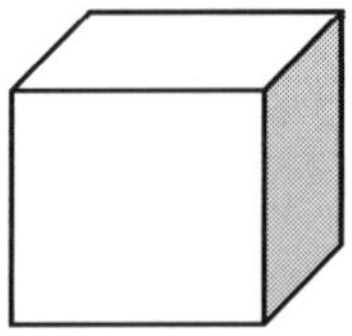

Rectangular Prisms

- A rectangular prism is a solid 3-dimensional object which has six rectangular faces.
- Volume of a Rectangular prism $= \boldsymbol{Length} \times \boldsymbol{Width} \times \boldsymbol{Height}$

$Volume = l \times w \times h$

$Surface\ area = 2 \times (wh + lw + lh)$

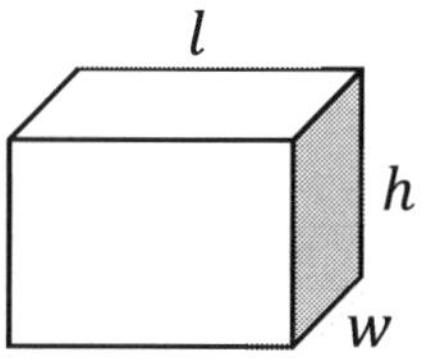

Examples:

1) Find the volume and surface area of the following rectangular prism.

Solution:

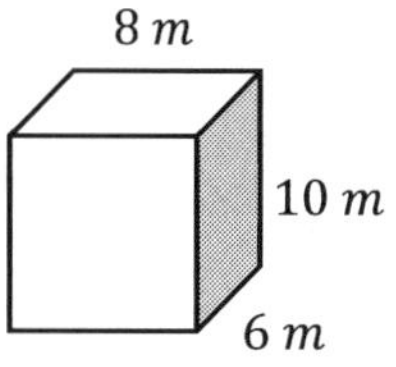

Use volume formula: $Volume = l \times w \times h$

Then: $Volume = 8 \times 6 \times 10 = 480\ m^3$

Use surface area formula: $Surface\ area = 2 \times (wh + lw + lh)$

Then: $Surface\ area = 2 \times \big((6 \times 10) + (8 \times 6) + (8 \times 10)\big)$

$= 2 \times (60 + 48 + 80) = 2 \times (188) = 376\ m^2$

2) Find the volume and surface area of rectangular prism.

Solution:

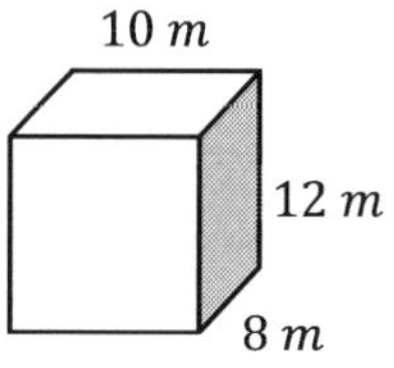

Use volume formula: $Volume = l \times w \times h$

Then: $Volume = 10 \times 8 \times 12 = 960\ m^3$

Use surface area formula: $Surface\ area = 2 \times (wh + lw + lh)$

Then: $Surface\ area = 2 \times \big((8 \times 12) + (10 \times 8) + (10 \times 12)\big)$

$= 2 \times (96 + 80 + 120) = 2 \times (296) = 592\ m^2$

Cylinder

- A cylinder is a solid geometric figure with straight parallel sides and a circular or oval cross section.
- $Volume\ of\ a\ Cylinder = \pi(radius)^2 \times height,\ \pi \approx 3.14$
- $Surface\ area\ of\ a\ cylinder = 2\pi r^2 + 2\pi rh$

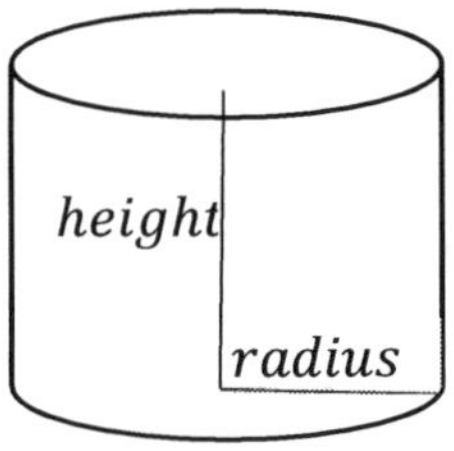

Examples:

1) *Find the volume and Surface area of the follow Cylinder.*

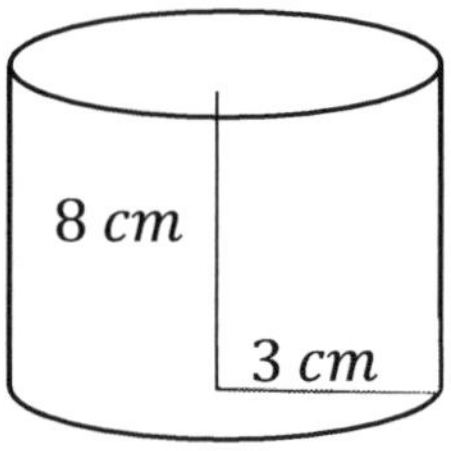

Solution:

Use volume formula: $Volume = \pi(radius)^2 \times height$
Then: $Volume = \pi(3)^2 \times 8 = 9\pi \times 8 = 72\pi$
$\pi = 3.14$ **then:** $Volume = 72\pi = 72 \times 3.14 = 226.08\ cm^3$
Use surface area formula: $Surface\ area = 2\pi r^2 + 2\pi rh$
Then: $2\pi(3)^2 + 2\pi(3)(8) = 2\pi(9) + 2\pi(24) = 18\pi + 48\pi = 66\pi$
$\pi = 3.14$ Then: $Surface\ area = 66 \times 3.14 = 207.24\ cm^2$

2) *Find the volume and Surface area of the follow Cylinder.*

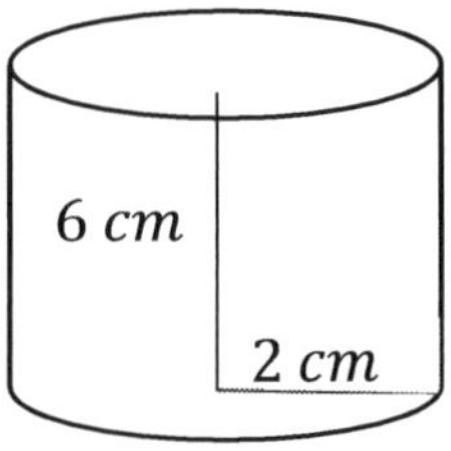

Solution:

Use volume formula: $Volume = \pi(radius)^2 \times height$
Then: $Volume = \pi(2)^2 \times 6 = \pi 4 \times 6 = 24\pi$
$\pi = 3.14$ **then:** $Volume = 24\pi = 75.36\ cm^3$
Use surface area formula: $Surface\ area = 2\pi r^2 + 2\pi rh$
Then: $= 2\pi(2)^2 + 2\pi(2)(6) = 2\pi(4) + 2\pi(12) = 8\pi + 24\pi = 32\pi$
$\pi = 3.14$ **then:** $Surface\ area = 32 \times 3.14 = 100.48\ cm^2$

Chapter 11: Practices

Find the missing side?

1)

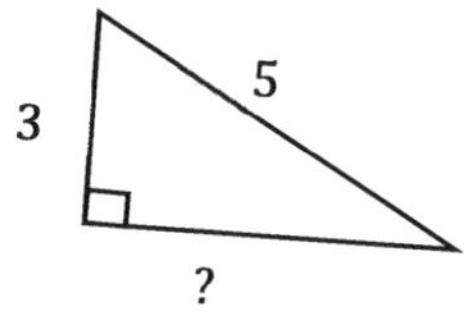

2)

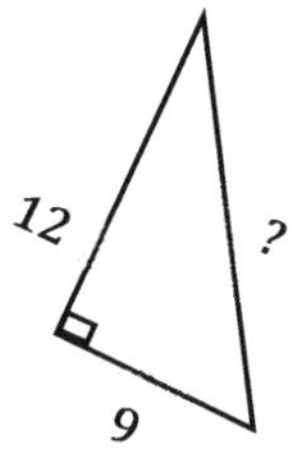

3)

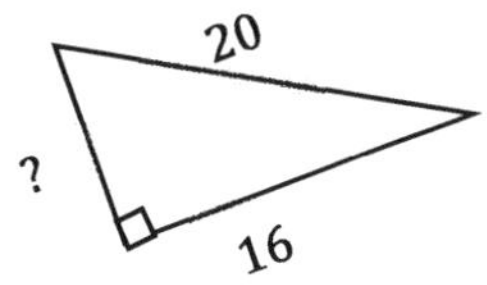

4)

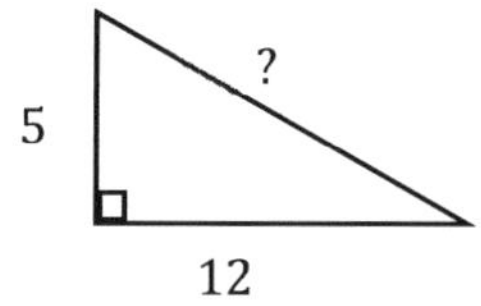

Find the measure of the unknown angle in each triangle.

5)

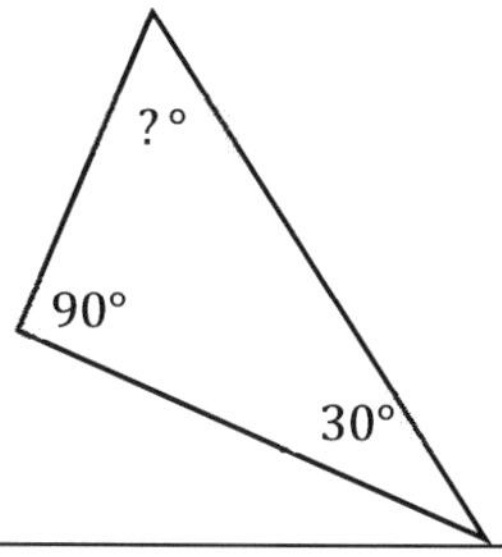

6)

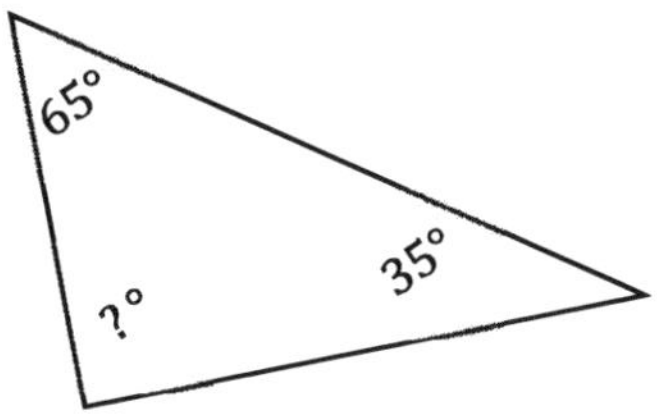

7)

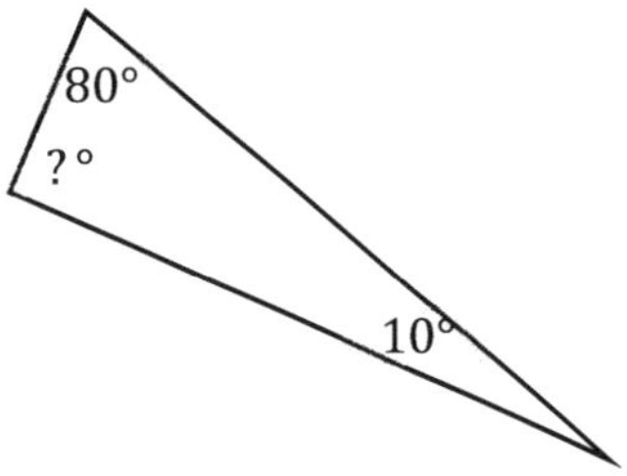

8)

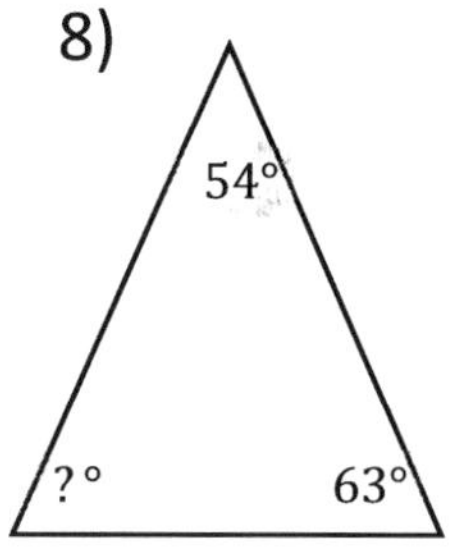

Find area of each triangle.

9)

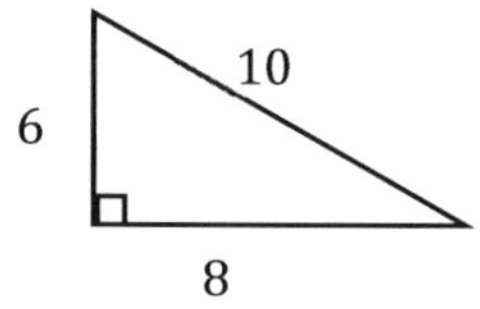

10)

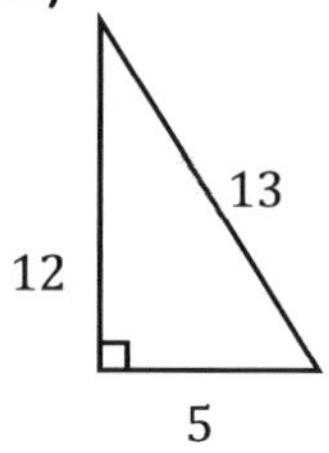

11)

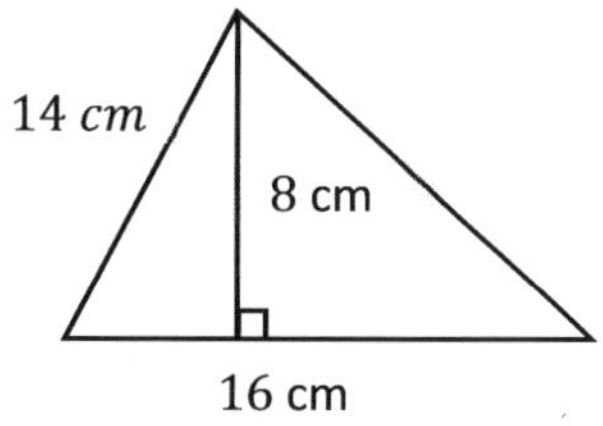

12)

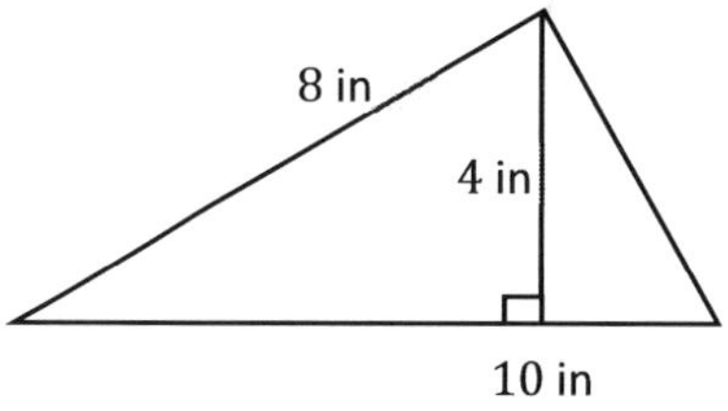

Find the perimeter of each shape.

13)

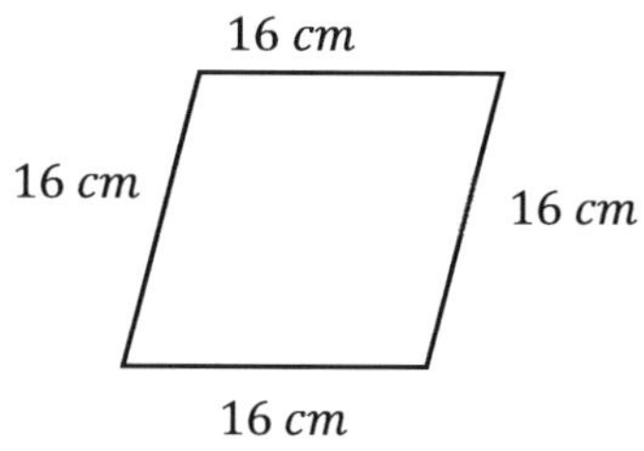

14)

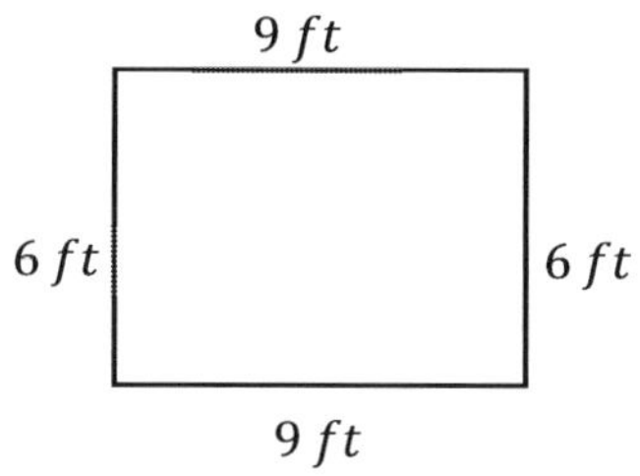

15)

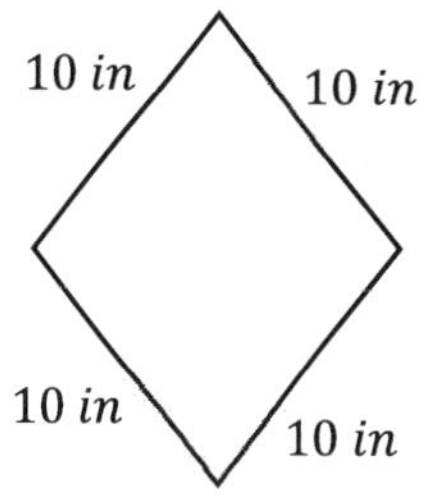

16)

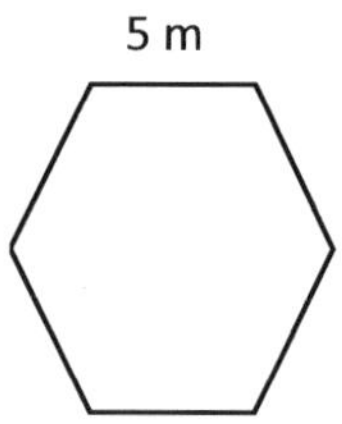

Complete the table below. ($\pi = 3.14$)

17)

	Radius	Diameter	Circumference	Area
Circle 1	3 *inches*	6 *inches*	18.84 *inches*	28.26 *square inches*
Circle 2			43.96 *meters*	
Circle 3		8 *ft*		
Circle 4				78.5 *square miles*

Find the area of each trapezoid.

18)

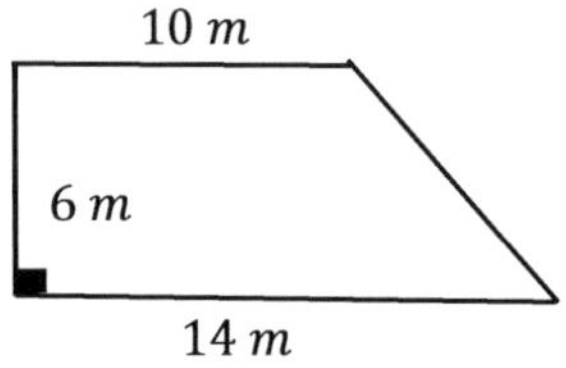

19)

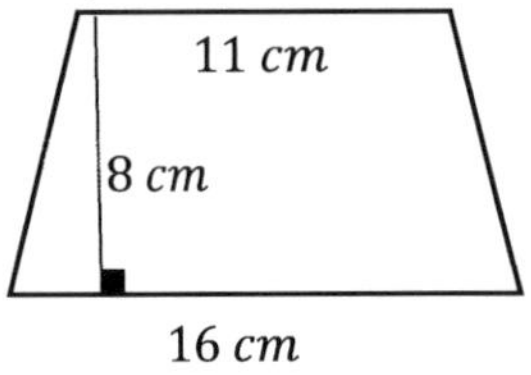

20)

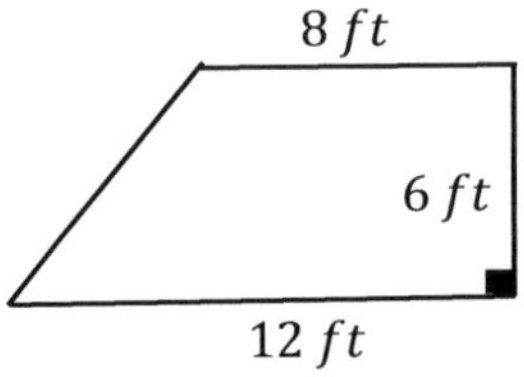

21)

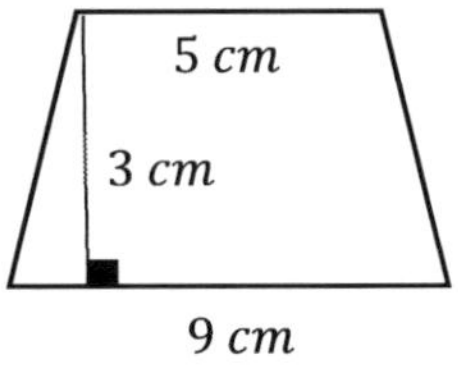

Find the volume of each cube.

22)

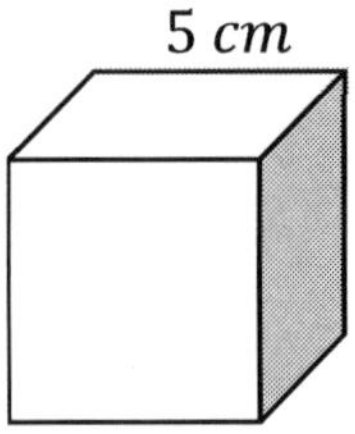

23)

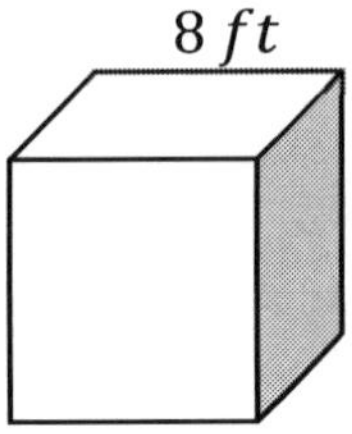

24)

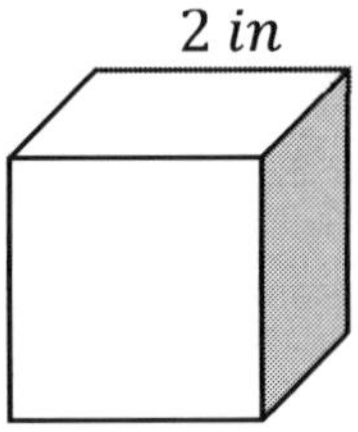

25)

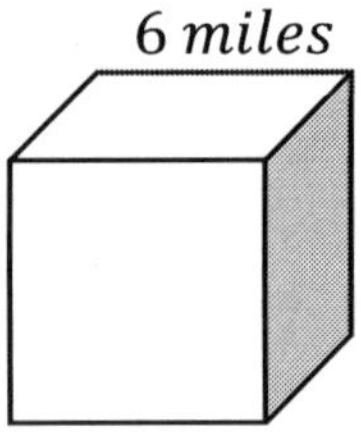

Find the volume of each Rectangular Prism.

26)

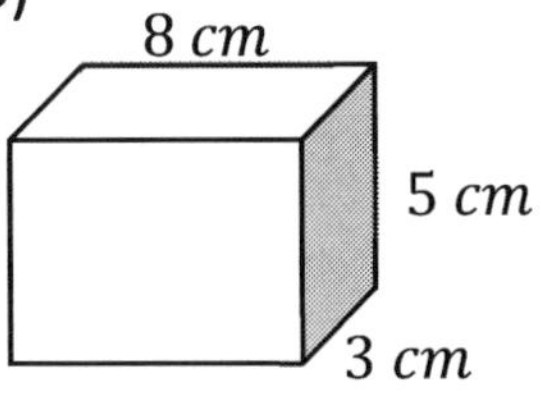

27)

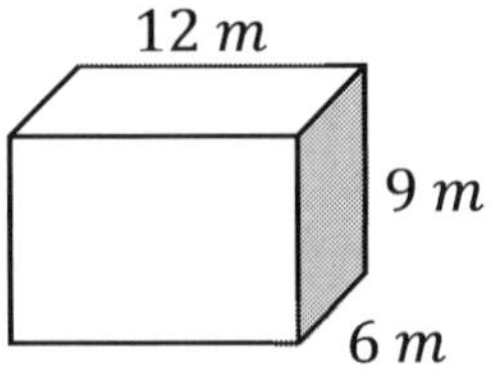

28)

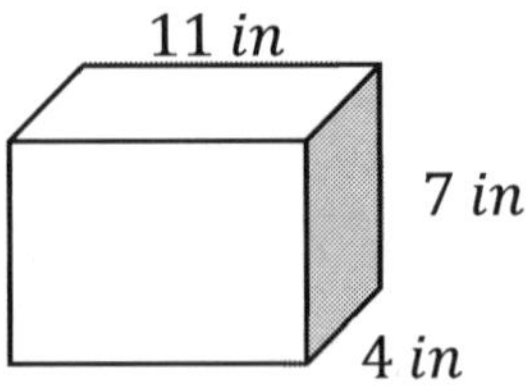

Find the volume of each Cylinder. Round your answer to the nearest tenth. $(\pi = 3.14)$

25)

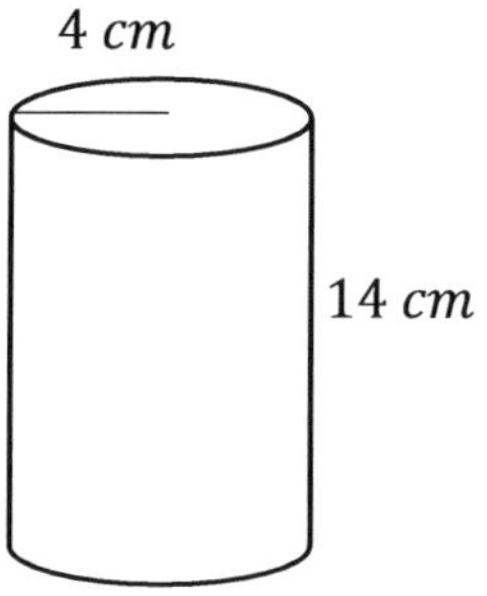

26)

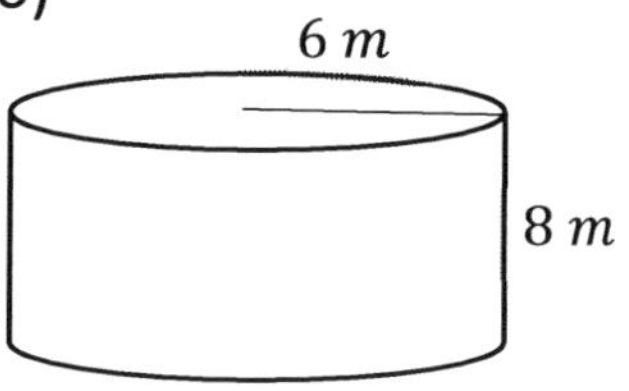

27)

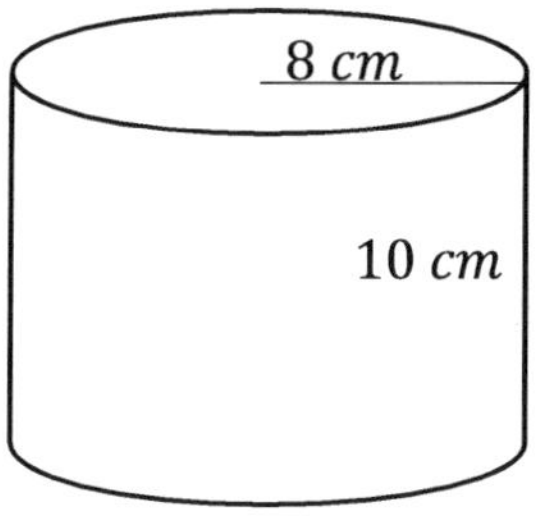

Answers – Chapter 11

1) 4
2) 15
3) 12
4) 13

5) 60°
6) 80°
7) 90°
8) 63°
9) 24 *square unites*
10) 30 *square unites*
11) 64 cm^2
12) 20 in^2

13) 64 *cm*
14) 30 *ft*
15) 40 *in*
16) 30 *m*

17)

	Radius	Diameter	Circumference	Area
Circle 1	3 *inches*	6 *inches*	18.84 *inches*	28.26 *square inches*
Circle 2	7 *meters*	14 *meters*	43.96 *meters*	153.86 *square meters*
Circle 3	4 *ft*	8 *ft*	25.12 *ft*	50.24 *square ft*
Circle 4	5 *miles*	10 *miles*	31.4 *miles*	78.5 *square miles*

18) 72 m^2
19) 108 cm^2
20) 60 ft^2
21) 21 cm^2

22) 125 cm^3
23) 512 ft^3
24) 8 in^3
25) 216 $miles^3$

26) 120 cm^3
27) 648 m^3
28) 308 in^3

29) 703.36 cm^3
30) 904.32 m^3
31) 2,009.6 cm^3

Chapter 12:

Statistics

Math Topics that you'll learn in this Chapter:

- ✓ Mean, Median, Mode, and Range of the Given Data
- ✓ Pie Graph
- ✓ Probability Problems
- ✓ Permutations and Combinations

Mean, Median, Mode, and Range of the Given Data

- Mean: $\frac{sum\ of\ the\ data}{total\ number\ of\ data\ entires}$
- Mode: the value in the list that appears most often
- Median: is the middle number of a group of numbers that have been arranged in order by size.
- Range: the difference of largest value and smallest value in the list

Examples:

1) What is the mode of these numbers? $4, 5, 7, 5, 7, 4, 0, 4$

Solution: Mode: the value in the list that appears most often.
Therefore, the mode is number 4. There are three number 4 in the data.

2) What is the median of these numbers? $5, 10, 14, 9, 16, 19, 6$

Solution: Write the numbers in order: $5, 6, 9, 10, 14, 16, 19$

Median is the number in the middle. Therefore, the median is 10.

3) What is the mean of these numbers? $8, 2, 8, 5, 3, 2, 4, 8$

Solution: Mean: $\frac{sum\ of\ the\ data}{total\ number\ of\ data\ entires} = \frac{8+2+8+5+3+2+4+8}{8} = 5$

4) What is the range in this list? $4, 9, 13, 8, 15, 18, 5$

Solution: Range is the difference of largest value and smallest value in the list. The largest value is 18 and the smallest value is 4. Then: $18 - 4 = 14$

Pie Graph

- A Pie Chart is a circle chart divided into sectors, each sector represents the relative size of each value.
- Pie charts represent a snapshot of how a group is broken down into smaller pieces.

Example:

A library has 820 books that include Mathematics, Physics, Chemistry, English and History. Use following graph to answer the questions.

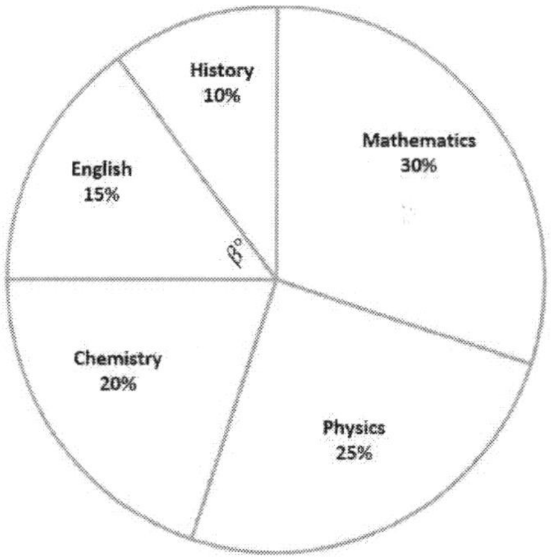

1) What is the number of Mathematics books?

Solution: Number of total books $= 820$

Percent of Mathematics books $= 30\% = 0.30$

Then, number of Mathematics books:

$$0.30 \times 820 = 246$$

2) What is the number of History books?

Solution: Number of total books $= 820$

Percent of History books $= 10\% = 0.10$

Then: $0.10 \times 820 = 82$

3) What is the number of Chemistry books?

Solution: Number of total books $= 820$

Percent of Chemistry books $= 20\% = 0.20$

Then: $0.20 \times 820 = 164$

Probability Problems

- ✓ Probability is the likelihood of something happening in the future. It is expressed as a number between zero (can never happen) to 1 (will always happen).
- ✓ Probability can be expressed as a fraction, a decimal, or a percent.
- ✓ Probability formula: $Probability = \frac{number\ of\ desired\ outcomes}{number\ of\ total\ outcomes}$

Examples:

1) Anita's trick-or-treat bag contains 12 pieces of chocolate, 18 suckers, 18 pieces of gum, 24 pieces of licorice. If she randomly pulls a piece of candy from her bag, what is the probability of her pulling out a piece of sucker?

   Solution: $\text{Probability} = \frac{number\ of\ desired\ outcomes}{\text{number of total outcomes}}$

   $\text{Probability of ulling out a piece of sucker} = \frac{18}{12+18+18+24} = \frac{18}{72} = \frac{1}{4}$

2) A bag contains 20 balls: four green, five black, eight blue, a brown, a red and one white. If 19 balls are removed from the bag at random, what is the probability that a brown ball has been removed?

   Solution: If 19 balls are removed from the bag at random, there will be one ball in the bag. The probability of choosing a brown ball is 1 out of 20. Therefore, the probability of not choosing a brown ball is 19 out of 20 and the probability of having not a brown ball after removing 19 balls is the same.

Permutations and Combinations

- Factorials are products, indicated by an exclamation mark. For example, $4! = 4 \times 3 \times 2 \times 1$(Remember that 0! is defined to be equal to 1.)
- Permutations: The number of ways to choose a sample of k elements from a set of n distinct objects where order does matter, and replacements are not allowed. For a permutation problem, use this formula:

$$_{n}P_{k} = \frac{n!}{(n-k)!}$$

- Combination: The number of ways to choose a sample of r elements from a set of n distinct objects where order does not matter, and replacements are not allowed. For a combination problem, use this formula:

$$_{n}C_{r} = \frac{n!}{r!\,(n-r)!}$$

Examples:

1) *How many ways can the first and second place be awarded to 8 people?*

Solution: Since the order matters, (the first and second place are different!) we need to use permutation formula where n is 10 and k is 2. Then: $\frac{n!}{(n-k)!} = \frac{8!}{(8-2)!} = \frac{8!}{6!} = \frac{8\times7\times6!}{6!}$, remove 6! from both sides of the fraction. Then: $\frac{8\times7\times6!}{6!} = 8 \times 7 = 56$

2) *How many ways can we pick a team of 2 people from a group of 6?*

Solution: Since the order doesn't matter, we need to use combination formula where n is 8 and r is 3. Then: $\frac{n!}{r!\,(n-r)!} = \frac{6!}{2!\,(6-2)!} = \frac{6!}{2!\,(4)!} = \frac{6\times5\times4!}{2!\,(4)!} = \frac{6\times5}{2\times1} = \frac{30}{2} = 15$

Chapter 12: Practices

Find the values of the Given Data.

1) $6, 12, 1, 1, 5$

Mode: _____ Range: _____

Mean: _____ Median: _____

2) $5, 8, 3, 7, 4, 3$

Mode: _____ Range: _____

Mean: _____ Median: _____

The circle graph below shows all Jason's expenses for last month. Jason spent $864 on his bills last month.

3) How much did Jason spend on his car last month? _________

4) How much did Jason spend for foods last month? _________

Jason's last month expenses

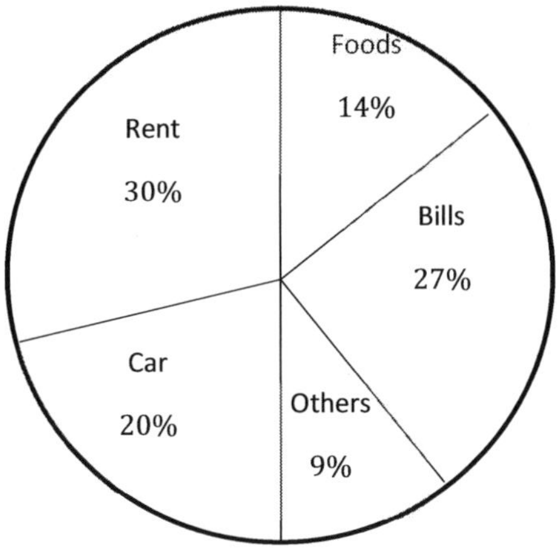

✍ ***Solve.***

5) Bag A contains 8 red marbles and 6 green marbles. Bag B contains 5 black marbles and 10 orange marbles. What is the probability of selecting a green marble at random from bag A? What is the probability of selecting a black marble at random from Bag B? __________ ______________

✍ ***Solve.***

6) Susan is baking cookies. She uses sugar, flour, butter, and eggs. How many different orders of ingredients can she try? ________________

7) Jason is planning for his vacation. He wants to go to museum, watch a movie, go to the beach, and play volleyball. How many different ways of ordering are there for him? ________________

8) In how many ways a team of 10 basketball players can to choose a captain and co-captain? ________________

9) How many ways can you give 3 balls to your 8 friends? ________________

10) A professor is going to arrange her 8 students in a straight line. In how many ways can she do this? ________________

Answers – Chapter 12

1) Mode: 1 , Range: 11, Mean: 5, Median: 5
2) Mode: 3 , Range: 5 , Mean: 5, Median: 4.5
3) $640
4) $448
5) $\frac{3}{7}, \frac{1}{3}$
6) 24
7) 24
8) 90
9) 56
10) 40,320

Chapter 13:

Functions Operations

Math Topics that you'll learn in this Chapter:

- ✓ Function Notation
- ✓ Adding and Subtracting Functions
- ✓ Multiplying and Dividing Functions
- ✓ Composition of Functions

Function Notation and Evaluation

- Functions are mathematical operations that assign unique outputs to given inputs.
- Function notation is the way a function is written. It is meant to be a precise way of giving information about the function without a rather lengthy written explanation.
- The most popular function notation is $f(x)$ which is read "f of x". Any letter can be used to name a function. for example: $g(x)$, $h(x)$, etc.
- To evaluate a function, plug in the input (the given value or expression) for the function's variable (place holder, x).

Examples:

1) Evaluate: $h(n) = n - 2$, find $h(2)$

Solution: Substitute n with 4: Then: $h(n) = n - 2 \rightarrow h(2) = (2)^2 - 2 \rightarrow h(2) = 4 - 2 = 2$

2) Evaluate: $w(x) = 5x - 1$, find $w(3)$.

Solution: Substitute x with 3: Then: $w(x) = 5x - 1 \rightarrow w(3) = 5(3) - 1 = 15 - 1 = 14$

3) Evaluate: $f(x) = x^2 - 2$, find $h(2)$.

Solution: Substitute x with 2: Then: $f(x) = x^2 - 2 \rightarrow f(2) = (2)^2 - 2 = 4 - 2 = 2$

4) Evaluate: $p(x) = 2x^2 - 4$, find $p(3a)$.

Solution: Substitute x with $3a$: Then: $p(x) = 2x^2 - 4 \rightarrow p(3a) = 2(3a)^2 - 4 \rightarrow$

$$p(3a) = 2(9a^2) - 4 = 18a^2 - 4$$

Adding and Subtracting Functions

- Just like we can add and subtract numbers and expressions, we can add or subtract two functions and simplify or evaluate them. The result is a new function.
- For two functions $f(x)$ and $g(x)$, we can create two new functions: $(f+g)(x) = f(x) + g(x)$ and $(f-g)(x) = f(x) - g(x)$

Examples:

1) $g(x) = a - 1, f(a) = a + 2$, Find: $(g + f)(a)$

   Solution: $(g + f)(a) = g(a) + f(a)$

   Then: $(g + f)(a) = (a - 1) + (a + 2) = 2a + 1$

2) $f(x) = 2x - 2, g(x) = x - 4$, Find: $(f - g)(x)$

   Solution: $(f - g)(x) = f(x) - g(x)$

   Then: $(f - g)(x) = (2x - 2) - (x - 4) = 2x - 2 - x + 4 = x + 2$

3) $g(x) = x^2 - 4, f(x) = 2x + 3$, Find: $(g + f)(x)$

   Solution: $(g + f)(x) = g(x) + f(x)$

   Then: $(g + f)(x) = (x^2 - 4) + (2x + 3) = x^2 + 2x - 1$

4) $f(x) = 2x^2 + 5, g(x) = 3x - 1$, Find: $(f - g)(5)$

   Solution: $(f - g)(x) = f(x) - g(x)$

   Then: $(f - g)(x) = (2x^2 + 5) - (3x - 1) = 2x^2 + 5 - 3x + 1 = 2x^2 - 3x + 6$

   Substitute x with 5: $(g - f)(5) = 2(5)^2 - 3(5) + 6 = 50 - 15 + 6 = 41$

Multiplying and Dividing Functions

- Just like we can multiply and divide numbers and expressions, we can multiply and divide two functions and simplify or evaluate them.
- For two functions $f(x)$ and $g(x)$, we can create two new functions:

$(f.g)(x) = f(x).g(x)$ and $\left(\frac{f}{g}\right)(x) = \frac{f(x)}{g(x)}$

Examples:

1) $g(x) = x - 2, f(x) = x + 3$, Find: $(g.f)(x)$

Solution: $(g.f)(x) = g(x).f(x) = (x - 2)(x + 3) = x^2 + 3x - 2x - 6$

2) $f(x) = x + 4, h(x) = x - 6$, Find: $\left(\frac{f}{h}\right)(x)$

Solution: $\left(\frac{f}{h}\right)(x) = \frac{f(x)}{h(x)} = \frac{x+4}{x-6}$

3) $g(x) = x + 5, f(x) = x - 2$, Find: $(g.f)(4)$

Solution: $(g.f)(x) = g(x).f(x) = (x + 5)(x - 2) = x^2 - 2x + 5x - 10 = x^2 + 3x - 10$

Substitute x with 4: $(g.f)(x) = (4)^2 + 3(4) - 10 = 16 + 12 - 10 = 18$

4) $f(x) = 2x + 3, h(x) = x + 8$, Find: $\left(\frac{f}{h}\right)(-1)$

Solution: $\left(\frac{f}{h}\right)(x) = \frac{f(x)}{h(x)} = \frac{2x+3}{x+8}$

Substitute x with -1: $\left(\frac{f}{h}\right)(x) = \frac{2x+3}{x+8} = \frac{2(-1)+3}{(-1)+8} = \frac{1}{7}$

Composition of Functions

- "Composition of functions" simply means combining two or more functions in a way where the output from one function becomes the input for the next function.
- The notation used for composition is: $(fog)(x) = f(g(x))$ and is read "f composed with g of x" or "f of g of x".

Examples:

1) Using $\text{f(x)} = \text{x} - 5$ *and* $\text{g(x)} = 2\text{x}$, *find:* $(\text{fog})(\text{x})$

Solution: $(fog)(x) = f\big(g(x)\big)$. Then: $(fog)(x) = f\big(g(x)\big) = f(2x)$

Now find $f(2x)$ by substituting x with $2x$ in $f(x)$ function. Then: $\text{f(x)} = \text{x} - 5$

$(x \to 2x) \to f(2x) = (2x) - 5 = 2x - 5$

2) *Using* $\text{f(x)} = \text{x} + 6$ *and* $\text{g(x)} = \text{x} - 2$, *find:* $(\text{g o f})(-1)$

Solution: $(f\ o\ g)(x) = f(g(x))$. *Then:* $(g\ o\ f)(x) = g\big(f(x)\big) = g(\text{x} + 6)$, *now substitute* x *in* g(x) *by* $(\text{x} + 6)$. *Then:* $g(\text{x} + 6) = (x + 6) - 2 = x + 6 - 2 = x + 4$

Substitute x with -1: $(g\ o\ f)(-1) = g\big(f(x)\big) = x + 4 = -1 + 4 = 3$

3) Using $\text{f(x)} = 2\text{x} - 2$ *and* $\text{g(x)} = 2\text{x}$, *find:* $f(g(5))$

Solution: First find $g(5))$: $\text{g(x)} = 2\text{x} \to \text{g}(5) = 2(5) = 10$

Then: $f\big(g(5)\big) = f(10)$. Now, find $f(10)$ by substituting x with 10 in $f(x)$ function.

Then: $f\big(g(5)\big) = f(10) = 2(10) - 2 = 20 - 2 = 18$

Chapter 13: Practices

Evaluate each function.

1) $g(n) = 6n - 3$, find $g(-2)$

_____

2) $h(x) = -8x + 12$, find $h(3)$

_____

3) $k(n) = 14 - 3n$, find $k(3)$

_____

4) $g(x) = 4x - 4$, find $g(-2)$

_____

5) $k(n) = 8n - 7$, find $k(4)$

_____

6) $w(n) = -2n + 14$, find $w(5)$

_____

Perform the indicated operation.

7) $f(x) = x + 6$

$g(x) = 3x + 3$

Find $(f - g)(2)$

_____

8) $g(x) = x - 3$

$f(x) = -x - 4$

Find $(g - f)(-2)$

_____

9) $h(t) = 5t + 4$

$g(t) = 2t + 2$

Find $(h + g)(-1)$

_____

10) $g(a) = 3a - 5$

$f(a) = a^2 + 6$

Find $(g + f)(3)$

_____

11) $g(x) = 4x - 5$

$h(x) = 6x^2 + 5$

Find $(g - f)(-2)$

_____

12) $h(x) = x^2 + 3$

$g(x) = -4x + 1$

Find $(h + g)(4)$

_____

Perform the indicated operation.

13) $g(x) = x + 2$

$f(x) = x + 3$

Find $(g.f)(4)$

_____

14) $f(x) = 2x$

$h(x) = -x + 6$

Find $(f.h)(-2)$

_____

15) $g(a) = a + 2$

$h(a) = 2a - 3$

Find $(g.h)(5)$

_____

16) $f(x) = 2x + 4$

$h(x) = 4x - 2$

Find $(\frac{f}{h})(2)$

_____

17) $f(x) = a^2 - 2$

$g(x) = -4 + 3a$

Find $(\frac{f}{g})(2)$

_____

18) $g(a) = 4a + 6$

$f(a) = 2a - 8$

Find $(\frac{g}{f})(3)$

_____

Using $f(x) = 2x + 5$ ***and*** $g(x) = x - 2$***, find:***

19) $g(f(2)) =$ ____

20) $g(f(-2)) =$ ____

21) $f(g(5)) =$ ____

22) $f(f(4)) =$ ____

23) $g(f(3)) =$ ____

24) $g(f(-3)) =$ ____

Answers – Chapter 13

1) -15
2) -12
3) 5
4) -12
5) 25
6) 4
7) -1
8) -3
9) -1
10) 19
11) -42
12) 4
13) 42
14) -32
15) 49
16) $\frac{4}{3}$
17) 1
18) -9
19) 7
20) -1
21) 11
22) 31
23) 9
24) -3

GED Test Review

The General Educational Development Test, commonly known as the GED or high school equivalency degree, is a standardized test and is the only high school equivalency test recognized in all 50 USA states.

Currently, GED is a computer-based test. Official computer-based tests are given at test centers all over the country. There are four subject area tests on GED:

- Reasoning Through Language Arts,
- Mathematical Reasoning,
- Social Studies,
- Science

The GED Mathematical Reasoning test is a 115-minute, single-section test that covers basic mathematics topics, quantitative problem-solving and algebraic questions. There are two parts on Mathematical Reasoning section. The first part contains 5 questions where calculators are not permitted. The second part contains 41 test questions. Calculator is allowed in the second part.

In this book, there are 2 complete GED Mathematical Reasoning Tests. Take these tests to see what score you'll be able to receive on a real GED test.

Good luck!

Time to refine your skill with a practice examination

Take a practice GED Math Test to simulate the test day experience. After you've finished, score your test using the answer key.

Before You Start

- You'll need a pencil and a calculator to take the test.
- There are two types of questions:

  Multiple choice questions: for each of these questions, there are four or more possible answers. Choose which one is best.

  Grid-ins questions: for these questions, write your answer in the box provided.
- It's okay to guess. You won't lose any points if you're wrong.
- The GED® Mathematical Reasoning test contains a formula sheet, which displays formulas relating to geometric measurement and certain algebra concepts. Formulas are provided to test- takers so that they may focus on application, rather than the memorization, of formulas.
- After you've finished the test, review the answer key to see where you went wrong and what areas you need to improve.

Good luck!

GED Mathematical Reasoning

Practice Test 1

2020 - 2021

Two Parts

Total number of questions: 46

Part 1 (Non-Calculator): 5 questions

Part 2 (Calculator): 41 questions

Total time for two parts: 115 Minutes

GED Test Mathematics Formula Sheet

Area of a:

Parallelogram	$A = bh$
Trapezoid	$A = \frac{1}{2}h(b_1 + b_2)$

Surface Area and Volume of a:

Rectangular/Right Prism	$SA = ph + 2B$	$V = Bh$
Cylinder	$SA = 2\pi rh + 2\pi r^2$	$V = \pi r^2 h$
Pyramid	$SA = \frac{1}{2}ps + B$	$V = \frac{1}{3}Bh$
Cone	$SA = \pi r + \pi r^2$	$V = \frac{1}{3}\pi r^2 h$
Sphere	$SA = 4\pi r^2$	$V = \frac{4}{3}\pi r^3$

(p = perimeter of base B; $\pi = 3.14$)

Algebra

Slope of a line	$m = \frac{y_2 - y_1}{x_2 - x_1}$
Slope-intercept form of the equation of a line	$y = mx + b$
Point-slope form of the Equation of a line	$y - y_1 = m(x - x_1)$
Standard form of a Quadratic equation	$y = ax^2 + bx + c$
Quadratic formula	$x = \frac{-b \pm \sqrt{b^2 - 4ac}}{2a}$
Pythagorean theorem	$a^2 + b^2 = c^2$
Simple interest	$I = prt$

(I = interest, p = principal, r = rate, t = time)

GED Mathematical Reasoning

Practice Test 1

Part 1 (Non-Calculator)

5 questions

Total time for two parts (Non-Calculator, and Calculator parts): 115 Minutes

You may NOT use a calculator on this part.

1) What is the value of this expression? $[3 \times (-14) - 48] - (-14) + [3 \times 8] \div 2$

Write your answer in the box below.

2) A tree 32 feet tall casts a shadow 12 feet long. Jack is 6 feet tall. How long is Jack's shadow?

☐A. $2.25\ ft$ ☐B. $4\ ft$

☐C. $4.25\ ft$ ☐D. $8\ ft$

3) What is the product of all possible values of x in the following equation?

$$|2x - 6| = 12$$

☐A. -27 ☐B. -3

☐C. 9 ☐D. 27

4) What is the slope of a line that is perpendicular to the line $3x - y = 6$?

☐A. -3 ☐B. $-\frac{1}{3}$

☐C. 2 ☐D. 6

5) What is the value of the expression $3(x - 2y) + (2 - x)^2$ when $x = 5$ and $= -3$?

☐A. -22 ☐B. 24

☐C. 42 ☐D. 88

GED Mathematical Reasoning

Practice Test 1

Part 2 (Calculator)

41 questions

Total time for two parts (Non-Calculator, and Calculator parts): 115 Minutes

You may use a calculator on this part.

6) If $x - 4(x + 2) = -15.5$, what is the value of x?

Write your answer in the box below.

7) Which of the following answers represents the compound inequality $-4 \leq 4x - 8 < 16$?

☐A. $-2 \leq x \leq 8$

☐B. $-2 < x \leq 8$

☐C. $1 < x \leq 6$

☐D. $1 \leq x < 6$

8) What is the volume of a box with the following dimensions?

Hight = $4\ cm$ Width = $5\ cm$ Length = $6\ cm$

☐A. $15\ cm^3$

☐B. $60\ cm^3$

☐C. $90\ cm^3$

☐D. $120\ cm^3$

9) Simplify the expression.

$$(6x^3 - 8x^2 + 2x^4) - (4x^2 - 2x^4 + 2x^3)$$

☐A. $4x^4 + 4x^3 - 12x^2$

☐B. $4x^3 - 12x^2$

☐C. $4x^4 + 4x^3 + 12x^2$

☐D. $8x^3 - 12x^2$

10) In two successive years, the population of a town is increased by 15% and 20%. What percent of the population is increased after two years?

☐A. 32%

☐B. 35%

☐C. 38%

☐D. 68%

11) Last week 24,000 fans attended a football match. This week three times as many bought tickets, but one sixth of them cancelled their tickets. How many are attending this week?

☐A. 48,000 ☐B. 54,000

☐C. 60,000 ☐D. 72,000

12) What is the perimeter of a square in centimeters that has an area of $595.36\ cm^2$?

Write your answer in the box below. (don't write the measurement)

13) Which of the following shows the numbers from least to greatest?

$$\frac{2}{3}, 0.68, 67\%, \frac{4}{5}$$

☐ A. $67\%, 0.68, \frac{2}{3}, \frac{4}{5}$ ☐B. $67\%, 0.68, \frac{4}{5}, \frac{2}{3}$

☐C. $0.68, 67\%, \frac{2}{3}, \frac{4}{5}$ ☐D. $\frac{2}{3}, 67\%, 0.68, \frac{4}{5}$

14) The mean of 50 test scores was calculated as 88. But, it turned out that one of the scores was misread as 94 but it was 69. What is the correct mean of the test scores?

☐A. 85 ☐B. 87

☐C. 87.5 ☐D. 88.5

15) Two dice are thrown simultaneously, what is the probability of getting a sum of 5 or 8?

☐A. $\frac{1}{3}$ ☐B. $\frac{1}{4}$

☐C. $\frac{1}{16}$ ☐D. $\frac{11}{36}$

16) A swimming pool holds 2,000 cubic feet of water. The swimming pool is 25 feet long and 10 feet wide. How deep is the swimming pool?

Write your answer in the box below. (Don't write the measurement)

17) Mr. Carlos family are choosing a menu for their reception. They have 3 choices of appetizers, 5 choices of entrees, 4 choices of cake. How many different menu combinations are possible for them to choose?

☐A. 12 ☐B. 32

☐C. 60 ☐D. 120

18) In a stadium the ratio of home fans to visiting fans in a crowd is 5: 7. Which of the following could be the total number of fans in the stadium? (Select one or more answer choices)

☐A. 12,324 ☐C. 42,326 ☐E. 66,812

☐B. 16,788 ☐D. 44,566

19) What is the area of a square whose diagonal is 8?

☐A. 16 ☐B. 32

☐C. 36 ☐D. 64

20) Anita's trick–or–treat bag contains 12 pieces of chocolate, 18 suckers, 18 pieces of gum, 24 pieces of licorice. If she randomly pulls a piece of candy from her bag, what is the probability of her pulling out a piece of sucker?

☐A. $\frac{1}{3}$ ☐B. $\frac{1}{4}$

☐C. $\frac{1}{6}$ ☐D. $\frac{1}{12}$

21) Which of the following points lies on the line $x + 2y = 4$? (Select one or more answer choices)

☐A. $(-2, 3)$ ☐B. $(1, 2)$

☐C. $(-1, 3)$ ☐D. $(-3, 4)$

☐E. $(0, 2)$

22) The perimeter of a rectangular yard is 60 meters. What is its length if its width is twice its length?

☐A. 10 meters ☐B. 18 meters

☐C. 20 meters ☐D. 24 meters

23) The average of 6 numbers is 12. The average of 4 of those numbers is 10. What is the average of the other two numbers.

☐A. 10 ☐B. 12

☐C. 14 ☐D. 16

24) What is the value of x in the following system of equations?

$$2x + 5y = 11$$
$$4x - 2y = -14$$

☐A. -1 ☐B. 1

☐C. -2 ☐D. 4

25) The perimeter of the trapezoid below is 36 cm. What is its area?

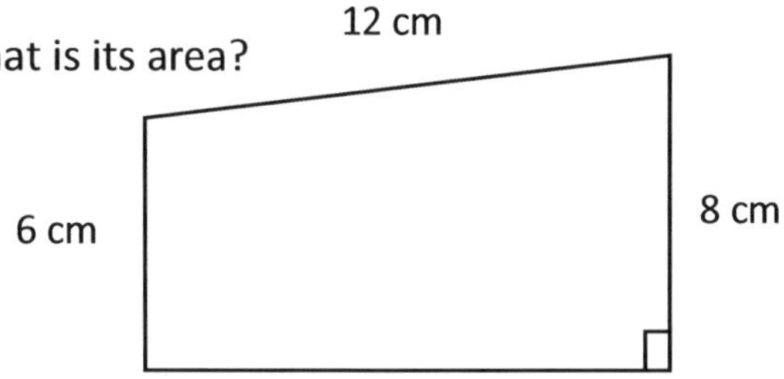

☐A. 576 cm^2 ☐B. 70 cm^2

☐C. 48 cm^2 ☐D. 24 cm^2

26) A card is drawn at random from a standard 52–card deck, what is the probability that the card is of Hearts? (The deck includes 13 of each suit clubs, diamonds, hearts, and spades)

☐A. $\frac{1}{3}$

☐B. $\frac{1}{4}$

☐C. $\frac{1}{6}$

☐D. $\frac{1}{52}$

27) The average of five numbers is 25. If a sixth number that is greater than 42 is added, then, which of the following could be the new average? (Select one or more answer choices)

☐A. 25

☐B. 26

☐C. 27

☐D. 28

☐E. 42

28) The diagonal of a rectangle is 10 inches long and the height of the rectangle is 8 inches. What is the perimeter of the rectangle in inches?

Write your answer in the box below.

29) The ratio of boys and girls in a class is 4: 7. If there are 44 students in the class, how many more boys should be enrolled to make the ratio 1: 1?

☐A. 8

☐B. 10

☐C. 12

☐D. 14

30) Mr. Jones saves $2,500 out of his monthly family income of $55,000. What fractional part of his income does he save?

☐A. $\frac{1}{22}$

☐B. $\frac{1}{11}$

☐C. $\frac{3}{25}$

☐D. $\frac{2}{15}$

31) Jason needs an 75% average in his writing class to pass. On his first 4 exams, he earned scores of 68%, 72%, 85%, and 90%. What is the minimum score Jason can earn on his fifth and final test to pass?

Write your answer in the box below.

$\square$

32) What is the value of x in the following equation? $\frac{2}{3}x + \frac{1}{6} = \frac{1}{3}$

☐A. 6 ☐B. $\frac{1}{2}$

☐C. $\frac{1}{3}$ ☐D. $\frac{1}{4}$

33) A bank is offering 3.5% simple interest on a savings account. If you deposit $12,000, how much interest will you earn in two years?

☐A. $420 ☐B. $840

☐C. $4200 ☐D. $8,400

34) Simplify $6x^2y^3(2x^2y)^3 =$

☐A. $12x^4y^6$ ☐B. $12x^8y^6$

☐C. $48x^4y^6$ ☐D. $48x^8y^6$

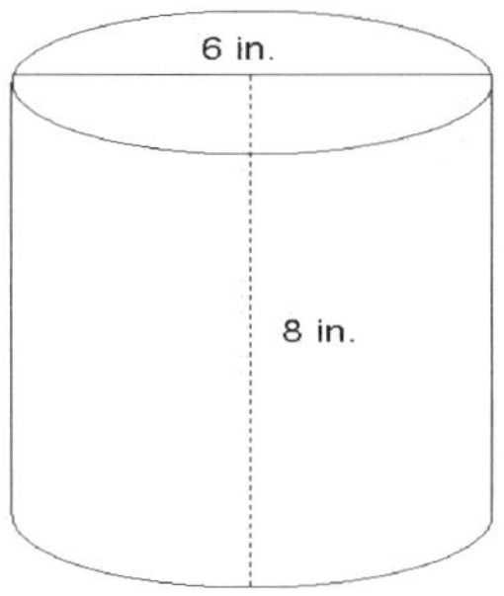

35) What is the surface area of the cylinder below?

☐A. $48\,\pi\,in^2$ ☐B. $57\,\pi\,in^2$

☐C. $66\,\pi\,in^2$ ☐D. $288\,\pi\,in^2$

36) The square of a number is $\frac{25}{64}$. What is the cube of that number?

☐A. $\frac{5}{8}$ ☐B. $\frac{25}{254}$

☐C. $\frac{125}{512}$ ☐D. $\frac{125}{64}$

37) What is the median of these numbers? $2, 27, 28, 19, 67, 44, 35$

☐A. 19 ☐B. 28

☐C. 44 ☐D. 35

38) A cruise line ship left Port A and traveled 80 miles due west and then 150 miles due north. At this point, what is the shortest distance from the cruise to port A in miles?

Write your answer in the box below.

39) What is the equivalent temperature of $104°F$ in Celsius? $C = \frac{5}{9}(F - 32)$

☐A. 32 ☐B. 40

☐C. 48 ☐D. 52

40) If 40% of a number is 4, what is the number?

☐A. 4 ☐B. 8

☐C. 10 ☐D. 12

41) The circle graph below shows all Mr. Green's expenses for last month. If he spent $\$660$ on his car, how much did he spend for his rent?

☐A. $\$700$ ☐B. $\$740$

☐C. $\$780$ ☐D. $\$810$

Mr. Green's monthly expenses

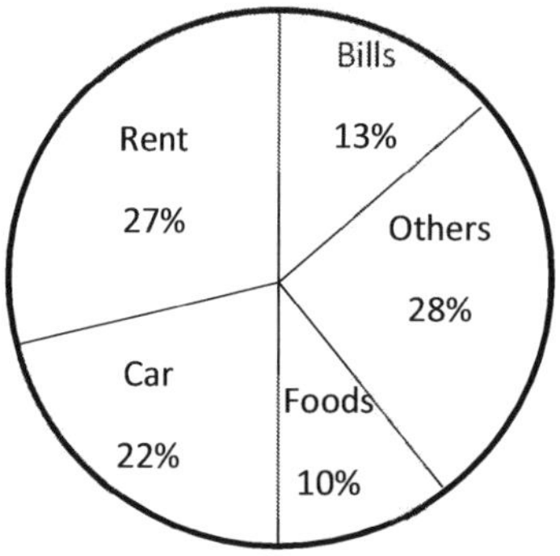

42) Jason is 9 miles ahead of Joe running at 5.5 miles per hour and Joe is running at the speed of 7 miles per hour. How long does it take Joe to catch Jason?

☐A. 3 *hours* ☐B. 4 *hours*

☐C. 6 *hours* ☐D. 8 *hours*

43) 55 students took an exam and 11 of them failed. What percent of the students passed the exam?

☐A. 20% ☐B. 40%

☐C. 60% ☐D. 80%

44) If 150% of a number is 75, then what is the 90% of that number?

☐A. 45 ☐B. 50

☐C. 70 ☐D.85

45) What is the slope of the line? $4x - 2y = 6$

Write your answer in the box below.

46) A football team had $20,000 to spend on supplies. The team spent $14,000 on new balls. New sport shoes cost $120 each. Which of the following inequalities represent the number of new shoes the team can purchase.

☐A. $120x + 14{,}000 \leq 20{,}000$

☐B. $120x + 14{,}000 \geq 20{,}000$

☐C. $14{,}000x + 120 \leq 20{,}000$

☐D. $14{,}000x + 12{,}0 \geq 20{,}000$

End of GED Mathematical Reasoning Practice Test 1.

GED Mathematical Reasoning

Practice Test 2

2020 - 2021

Two Parts

Total number of questions: 46

Part 1 (Non-Calculator): 5 questions

Part 2 (Calculator): 41 questions

Total time for two parts: 115 Minutes

GED Test Mathematics Formula Sheet

Area of a:

Parallelogram	$A = bh$
Trapezoid	$A = \frac{1}{2}h(b_1 + b_2)$

Surface Area and Volume of a:

Rectangular/Right Prism	$SA = ph + 2B$	$V = Bh$
Cylinder	$SA = 2\pi rh + 2\pi r^2$	$V = \pi r^2 h$
Pyramid	$SA = \frac{1}{2}ps + B$	$V = \frac{1}{3}Bh$
Cone	$SA = \pi r + \pi r^2$	$V = \frac{1}{3}\pi r^2 h$
Sphere	$SA = 4\pi r^2$	$V = \frac{4}{3}\pi r^3$

(p = perimeter of base B; $\pi = 3.14$)

Algebra

Slope of a line	$m = \frac{y_2 - y_1}{x_2 - x_1}$
Slope-intercept form of the equation of a line	$y = mx + b$
Point-slope form of the Equation of a line	$y - y_1 = m(x - x_1)$
Standard form of a Quadratic equation	$y = ax^2 + bx + c$
Quadratic formula	$x = \frac{-b \pm \sqrt{b^2 - 4ac}}{2a}$
Pythagorean theorem	$a^2 + b^2 = c^2$
Simple interest	$I = prt$

(I = interest, p = principal, r = rate, t = time)

GED Mathematical Reasoning

Practice Test 2

Part 1 (Non-Calculator)

5 questions

Total time for two parts (Non-Calculator, and Calculator parts): 115 Minutes

You may NOT use a calculator on this part.

1) Which of the following is the same as: 0.000 000 000 000 042 121?

☐A. 4.2121×10^{14}

☐B. 4.2121×10^{-14}

☐C. $42{,}121 \times 10^{-10}$

☐D. 42.121×10^{-13}

2) 5 less than twice a positive integer is 83. What is the integer?

☐A.39

☐B.41

☐C.42

☐D.44

3) A shirt costing \$200 is discounted 15%. After a month, the shirt is discounted another 15%. Which of the following expressions can be used to find the selling price of the shirt?

☐A. $(200)(0.70)$

☐B. $(200) - 200(0.30)$

☐C. $(200)(0.15) - (200)(0.15)$

☐D. $(200)(0.85)(0.85)$

4) Which of the following points lies on the line $2x + 4y = 10$

☐A. $(2, 1)$

☐B. $(-1, 3)$

☐C. $(-2, 2)$

☐D. $(2, 2)$

5) What is the value of the expression? $5 + 8 \times (-2) - [4 + 22 \times 5] \div 6$

Write your answer in the box below.

GED Mathematical Reasoning

Practice Test 2

Part 2 (Calculator)

41 questions

Total time for two parts (Non-Calculator, and Calculator parts): 115 Minutes

You may use a calculator on this part.

6) A student gets an 85% on a test with 40 questions. How many answers did the student solve correctly?

☐ A.25 ☐B. 28

☐ C.34 ☐D. 36

7) The width of a box is one third of its length. The height of the box is one third of its width. If the length of the box is 27 cm, what is the volume of the box?

☐A.81 cm^3 ☐ B. 162 cm^3

☐C. 243cm^3 ☐ D. 729 cm^3

8) If 60% of A is 30% of B, then B is what percent of A?

☐A. 3% ☐B. 30%

☐ C. 200% ☐D. 300%

9) How many possible outfit combinations come from six shirts, three slacks, and five ties?

Write your answer in the box below.

10) A ladder leans against a wall forming a 60° angle between the ground and the ladder. If the bottom of the ladder is 30 feet away from the wall, how long is the ladder?

☐A.30 $feet$ ☐B. 40 $feet$

☐C. 50 $feet$ ☐D. 60 $feet$

11) When a number is subtracted from 24 and the difference is divided by that number, the result is 3. What is the value of the number?

☐A.2 ☐B. 4

☐C. 6 ☐D.12

12) An angle is equal to one fifth of its supplement. What is the measure of that angle in degrees?

☐A. 20° ☐B. 30°

☐ C. 45° ☐D. 60°

13) John traveled $150\ km$ in 6 hours and Alice traveled $180\ km$ in 4 hours. What is the ratio of the average speed of John to average speed of Alice?

☐A. $3 : 2$ ☐B. $2 : 3$

☐C. $5 : 9$ ☐D. $5 : 6$

14) If 40% of a class are girls, and 25% of girls play tennis, what percent of the class play tennis?

☐A. 10% ☐B. 15%

☐C. 20% ☐D. 40%

15) What is the value of y in the following system of equation?

$$3x - 4y = -40$$

$$-x + 2y = 10$$

Write your answer in the box below.

☐

16) In five successive hours, a car travels $40\ km$, $45\ km$, $50\ km$, $35\ km$ and $55\ km$. In the next five hours, it travels with an average speed of $50\ km\ per\ hour$. Find the total distance the car traveled in 10 hours.

☐A. $425\ km$ ☐B. $450\ km$

☐C. $475\ km$ ☐D. $500\ km$

17) How long does a 420–miles trip take moving at 50 miles per hour (mph)?

☐A. $4\ hours$ ☐B. $6\ hours\ and\ 24\ minutes$

☐C. $8\ hours\ and\ 24\ minutes$ ☐D. $8\ hours\ and\ 30\ minutes$

18) In a bag there are only red marbles and blue marbles. The ratio of red marbles to blue marbles is $2:5$. Which of the following could be the total number of marbles in the bag? (Select one or more answer choices)

☐A. 324 ☐C. 826 ☐E. 662

☐B. 688 ☐D. 596

19) Which of the following points lies on the line $3x + 2y = 11$? (Select one or more answer choices)

☐A. $(-1, 3)$ ☐C. $(-1, 7)$ ☐E. $(0, 2)$

☐B. $(2, 3)$ ☐D. $(5, -2)$

20) Right triangle ABC has two legs of lengths $6\ cm$ (AB) and $8\ cm$ (AC). What is the length of the third side (BC)?

☐ A. $4\ cm$ ☐ B. $6\ cm$

☐ C. $8\ cm$ ☐ D. $10\ cm$

21) The ratio of boys to girls in a school is $2:3$. If there are 600 students in a school, how many boys are in the school.

Write your answer in the box below.

22) 25 is What percent of 20?

☐A. 20% ☐B. 25%

☐C. 125% ☐D. 150%

23) The perimeter of the trapezoid below is 54. What is its area?

Write your answer in the box below.

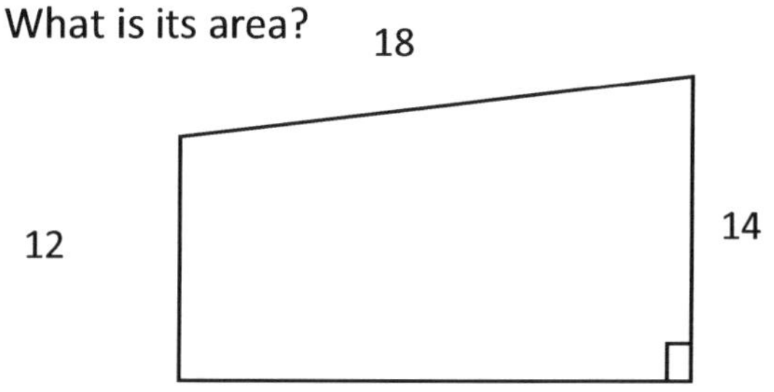

24) Two third of 18 is equal to $\frac{2}{5}$ of what number?

☐A. 12 ☐B. 20

☐C. 30 ☐D. 60

25) The marked price of a computer is D dollar. Its price decreased by 20% in January and later increased by 10% in February. What is the final price of the computer in D dollar?

☐A. 0.80 D ☐B. 0.88 D

☐C. 0.90 D ☐D. 1.20 D

26) The area of a circle is 64 π. What is the circumference of the circle?

☐A. 8 π ☐B. 16 π

☐C. 32 π ☐D. 64 π

27) A $40 shirt now selling for $28 is discounted by what percent?

☐A. 20% ☐B. 30%

☐C. 40% ☐D. 60%

28) In 1999, the average worker's income increased $2,000 per year starting from $24,000 annual salary. Which equation represents income greater than average? (I = income, x = number of years after 1999)

☐A. $I > 2{,}000\,x + 24{,}000$ ☐B. $I > -2{,}000\,x + 24{,}000$

☐C. $I < -2000\,x + 24{,}000$ ☐D. $I < 2{,}000\,x - 24{,}000$

29) From last year, the price of gasoline has increased from $\$1.25$ per gallon to $\$1.75$ per gallon. The new price is what percent of the original price?

☐A. 72% ☐B. 120%

☐C. 140% ☐D. 160%

30) A boat sails 40 miles south and then 30 miles east. How far is the boat from its start point?

☐A. $45\ miles$ ☐B. $50\ miles$

☐C. $60\ miles$ ☐D. $70\ miles$

31) Which of the following could be the product of two consecutive prime numbers?

☐A. 2 ☐B. 10

☐C. 14 ☐D. 15

32) Jason purchased a laptop for $\$529.72$. The laptop is regularly priced at $\$646.00$. What was the percent discount Jason received on the laptop?

☐A. 12% ☐B. 18%

☐C. 20% ☐D. 25%

33) The score of Emma was half as that of Ava and the score of Mia was twice that of Ava. If the score of Mia was 40, what is the score of Emma?

☐A. 5 ☐B. 10

☐C. 20 ☐D. 40

34) A bag contains 18 balls: two green, five black, eight blue, a brown, a red and one white. If 17 balls are removed from the bag at random, what is the probability that a brown ball has been removed?

☐A. $\frac{1}{9}$ ☐B. $\frac{1}{6}$

☐C. $\frac{16}{17}$ ☐D. $\frac{17}{18}$

35) The average of five consecutive numbers is 38. What is the smallest number?

☐A. 38 ☐B. 36

☐C. 34 ☐D. 12

36) How many tiles of 8 cm^2 is needed to cover a floor of dimension 8 cm by 24 cm?

☐A. 6 ☐B. 12

☐C. 18 ☐D. 24

37) A rope weighs 600 grams per meter of length. What is the weight in kilograms of 12.2 meters of this rope? ($1\ kilograms = 1{,}000\ grams$)

☐A. 0.0732 ☐B. 0.732

☐C. 7.32 ☐D. 7.320

38) A chemical solution contains 4% alcohol. If there is 32 ml of alcohol, what is the volume of the solution?

☐A. 240 ml ☐B. 480 ml

☐C. 800 ml ☐D. 1200 ml

39) The average weight of 23 girls in a class is 60 kg and the average weight of 32 boys in the same class is 62 kg. What is the average weight of all the 55 students in that class?

☐A. 60 ☐B. 61.16

☐C. 61.68 ☐D. 62.90

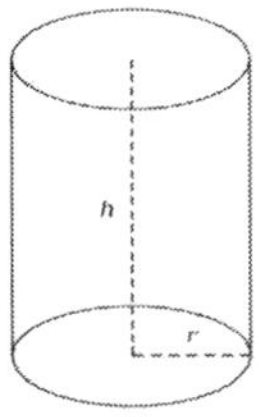

40) The price of a laptop is decreased by 20% to \$360. What is its original price?

☐A. 320 ☐B. 380

☐C. 400 ☐D. 450

41) What is the median of these numbers? 3, 10, 13, 8, 15, 19, 5

☐A. 8 ☐B. 10

☐C. 13 ☐D. 15

42) The radius of the following cylinder is 6 inches and its height is 12 inches. What is the surface area of the cylinder in square inches?

Write your answer in the box below. (π equals 3.14)

43) The average of 13, 15, 20 and x is 15. What is the value of x?

Write your answer in the box below.

44) The price of a sofa is decreased by 25% to $\$420$. What was its original price?

☐A. $\$480$ ☐B. $\$520$

☐C. $\$560$ ☐D. $\$600$

45) In the xy-plane, the point $(1, 2)$ and $(-1,6)$ are on line A. Which of the following points could also be on line A? (Select one or more answer choices)

☐A. $(-1, 2)$ ☐D. $(3, -2)$

☐B. $(5, 7)$ ☐E. $(6, -8)$

☐C. $(3, 4)$

46) A bank is offering 4.5% simple interest on a savings account. If you deposit $\$9{,}000$, how much interest will you earn in five years?

☐A. $\$405$ ☐B. $\$720$

☐C. $\$2{,}025$ ☐D. $\$3{,}600$

End of GED Mathematical Reasoning Practice Test 2.

GED Mathematical Reasoning Practice Tests

Answer Keys

Now, it's time to review your results to see where you went wrong and what areas you need to improve.

GED Math Practice Test 1

1	-64	**21**	A, E	**41**	D
2	A	**22**	A	**42**	C
3	A	**23**	D	**43**	D
4	B	**24**	C	**44**	A
5	C	**25**	B	**45**	2
6	2.5	**26**	B	**46**	A
7	D	**27**	D, E		
8	D	**28**	28		
9	A	**29**	C		
10	C	**30**	A		
11	C	**31**	60		
12	97.6	**32**	D		
13	D	**33**	B		
14	C	**34**	D		
15	B	**35**	C		
16	8	**36**	C		
17	C	**37**	B		
18	A, B	**38**	170		
19	B	**39**	B		
20	B	**40**	C		

GED Math Practice Test 2

1	B	**21**	240	**41**	B
2	D	**22**	C	**42**	678.24
3	D	**23**	130	**43**	12
4	B	**24**	C	**44**	C
5	-30	**25**	B	**45**	D, E
6	C	**26**	B	**46**	C
7	D	**27**	B		
8	C	**28**	A		
9	90	**29**	C		
10	D	**30**	B		
11	C	**31**	D		
12	B	**32**	B		
13	C	**33**	B		
14	A	**34**	D		
15	-5	**35**	B		
16	C	**36**	D		
17	C	**37**	C		
18	C, E	**38**	C		
19	C, D	**39**	B		
20	D	**40**	D		

How to score your test

Each GED area test is scored on a scale of 100 - 200 points. To pass the GED, you must earn at least 145 on each of the four subject tests, for a total of at least 580 points (out of a possible 800).

Each subject test should be passed individually. It means that you must get 145 on each section of the test. If you failed one subject test but did well enough on another to get a total score of 580, that's still not a passing score.

There are four possible scores that you can receive on the GED Test:

Not Passing: This indicates that your score is lower than 145 on any of the four tests. If you do not pass, you can reschedule up to two times a year to retake any or all subjects of the GED test.

Passing Score/High School Equivalency: This score indicates that your score is between 145-164. Remember that points on one subject of the test do not carry over to the other subjects.

College Ready: This indicates that your score is between 165-175, demonstrating career and college readiness. A College Ready score shows that you may not need placement testing or remediation before beginning a college degree program.

College Ready + Credit: This indicates that your score is 175 or higher. This shows that you've already mastered some skills that would be taught in college courses. Depending on a school's policy, this can translate to some college credits–saving you time and money during your college education.

There are approximately 46 questions on GED Mathematical Reasoning. Similar to other subject areas, you will need a minimum score of 145 to pass the Mathematical Reasoning Test. There are 49 raw score points on the GED math test. The raw points correspond with correct answers. Most questions have one answer; therefore, they only have one point. There is more than one point for questions that have more than one answer. You'll get a raw score out of the 49 possible points. This will then be converted into your scaled score out of 200. Approximately, you need to get 32 out of 49 raw score to pass the Mathematical Reasoning section.

To score your GED Mathematical Reasoning practice tests, first find your raw score.

There were 46 questions on each GED Mathematical Reasoning practice test. All questions have one point except following questions that have 2 points:

GED Mathematical Reasoning practice test 1:

Question 18: Two points

Question 21: Two points

Question 27: Two points

GED Mathematical Reasoning practice test 2:

Question 18: Two points

Question 19: Two points

Question 45: Two points

Use the following table to convert GED Mathematical Reasoning raw score to scaled score.

GED Mathematical Reasoning raw score to scaled score	
Raw Scores	Scaled Scores
$Below\ 32\ (not\ passing)$	$Below\ 145$
$32 - 36$	$145 - 164$
$37 - 40$	$165 - 175$
$Above\ 40$	$Above\ 175$

GED Mathematical Reasoning Practice Tests Answers and Explanations

GED Mathematical Reasoning Practice Test 1

Answers and Explanations

1) The answer is: -64

Use PEMDAS (order of operation): $[3 \times (-14) - 48] — 14 + [3 \times 8] \div 2 =$

$$[-42 - 48] + 14 + 24 \div 2 = -90 + 14 + 12 = -64$$

2) Choice A is correct

Write a proportion and solve for the missing number. $\frac{32}{12} = \frac{6}{x} \rightarrow 32x = 6 \times 12 = 72$

$32x = 72 \rightarrow x = \frac{72}{32} = 2.25$

3) Choice A is correct

To solve absolute values equations, write two equations. $2x - 6$ can equal positive 12, or negative 12. Therefore, $2x - 6 = 12 \Rightarrow 2x = 18 \Rightarrow x = 9$.

$2x - 6 = -12 \Rightarrow 2x = -12 + 6 = -6 \Rightarrow x = -3$.

Find the product of solutions: $-3 \times 9 = -27$

4) Choice B is correct

The equation of a line in slope intercept form is: $y = \mathrm{m}x + b$. Solve for y. $3x - y = 6 \rightarrow$

$-y = -3x + 6$. Divide both sides by (-1). Then: $-y = -3x + 6 \rightarrow y = 3x - 6$

The slope of this line is 3. The product of the slopes of two perpendicular lines is -1. Therefore, the slope of a line that is perpendicular to this line is:

$$m_1 \times m_2 = -1 \Rightarrow 3 \times m_2 = -1 \Rightarrow m_2 = \frac{-1}{3} = -\frac{1}{3}$$

5) Choice C is correct

Plug in the value of x and y. $3(x - 2y) + (2 - x)^2$ when $x = 5$ and $y = -3$

$3(x - 2y) + (2 - x)^2 = 3(5 - 2(-3)) + (2 - 5)^2 = 3(5 + 6) + (-3)^2 = 33 + 9 = 42$

6) The answer is 2.5

First, use distribute property to simplify $-4(x+2)$. $\quad -4(x+2) = -4x - 8$

Now, combine like terms: $x - 4(x+2) = -15.5 \rightarrow x - 4x - 8 = -15.5 \rightarrow -3x - 8 = -15.5$

Add 8 to both sides of the equation: $-3x - 8 + 8 = -15.5 + 8 \rightarrow -3x = -7.5$. Divide both sides by -3. Then: $-3x = -7.5 \rightarrow \frac{-3x}{-3} = \frac{-7.5}{-3} \rightarrow x = 2.5$

7) Choice D is correct

Solve for x. $x - 4 \leq 4x - 8 < 16 \Rightarrow$ (add 8 all sides) $-4 + 8 < 4x - 8 + 8 < 16 + 8 \Rightarrow$

$4 < 4x < 24 \Rightarrow$ (divide all sides by 4) $1 \leq x < 6$

x is between 1 and 6. Choice D represents this inequality.

8) **Choice D is correct**

$Volume\ of\ a\ box = length \times width \times height = 4 \times 5 \times 6 = 120$

9) Choice A is correct

Simplify and combine like terms. $(6x^3 - 8x^2 + 2x^4) - (4x^2 - 2x^4 + 2x^3) \Rightarrow$
$(6x^3 - 8x^2 + 2x^4) - 4x^2 + 2x^4 - 2x^3 \Rightarrow 4x^4 + 4x^3 - 12x^2$

10) Choice C is correct

the population is increased by 15% and 20%. 15% increase changes the population to 115% of original population. For the second increase, multiply the result by 120%.

$(1.15) \times (1.20) = 1.38 = 138\%$. 38 percent of the population is increased after two years.

11) Choice C is correct

Three times of 24,000 is 72,000. One sixth of them cancelled their tickets.

One sixth of 72,000 equals 12,000 $(\frac{1}{6} \times 72{,}000 = 12{,}000)$.

60,000 $(72000 - 12{,}000 = 60{,}000)$ fans are attending this week

12) The answer is 97.6

The area of the square is 595.36. Therefore, the side of the square is square root of the area.

$\sqrt{595.36} = 24.4$. Four times the side of the square is the perimeter: $4 \times 24.4 = 97.6$

13) Choice D is correct

Change the numbers to decimal and then compare. $\frac{2}{3} = 0.666\ldots, 0.68, 67\% = 0.67, \frac{4}{5} = 0.80$

Therefore: $\frac{2}{3} < 67\% < 0.68 < \frac{4}{5}$

14) Choice C is correct

average (mean) $= \frac{\text{sum of terms}}{\text{number of terms}} \Rightarrow 88 = \frac{\text{sum of terms}}{50} \Rightarrow sum = 88 \times 50 = 4{,}400$

The difference of 94 and 69 is 25. Therefore, 25 should be subtracted from the sum.

$4400 - 25 = 4{,}375$, mean $\frac{\text{sum of terms}}{\text{number of terms}} \Rightarrow mean = \frac{4{,}375}{50} = 87.5$

15) Choice B is correct

For sum of 5: $(1\ \&\ 4)$ and $(4\ \&\ 1)$, $(2\ \&\ 3)$ and $(3\ \&\ 2)$, therefore we have 4 options.
For sum of 8: $(5\ \&\ 3)$ and $(3\ \&\ 5)$, $(4\ \&\ 4)$ and $(2\ \&\ 6)$, $and (6\ \&\ 2)$. There are 5 options. To get a sum of 5 or 8 for two dice: $4 + 5 = 9$
Since, we have $6 \times 6 = 36$ total number of options, the probability of getting a sum of 5 and 8 is 11 out of 36 or $\frac{11}{36} = \frac{1}{4}$

16) The answer is 8.

Use formula of rectangle prism volume. $V = (length)(width)(height) \Rightarrow$

$2000 = (25)(10)(height) \Rightarrow height = 2{,}000 \div 250 = 8$

17) Choice C is correct

To find the number of possible outfit combinations, multiply number of options for each factor:

$3 \times 5 \times 4 = 60$

18) Choices A and B are correct

(If you selected 3 choices and 2 of them are correct, then you get one point. If you answered 2 or 3 choices and one of them is correct, you receive one point. If you selected more than 3 choices, you won't get any point for this question.)

In the stadium the ratio of home fans to visiting fans in a crowd is 5: 7. Therefore, total number of fans must be divisible by 12: $5 + 7 = 12$.
Let's review the choices:

☐A. 12,324: $12{,}324 \div 12 = 1{,}027$

☐B. 16,788: $16{,}788 \div 12 = 1{,}399$

☐C. 42,326 $42{,}326 \div 12 = 3{,}527.166$

☐D. 44,566 $44{,}566 \div 12 = 3{,}713.833$

☐E. 66,812 $66{,}812 \div 12 = 5{,}567.66666$

Only choices A and B when divided by 12 result a whole number.

19) Choice B is correct

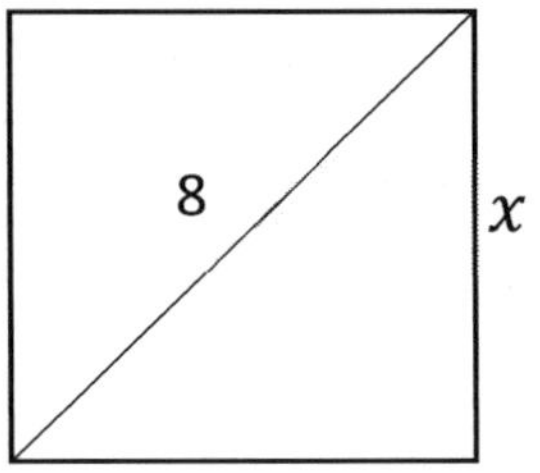

The diagonal of the square is 8. Let x be the side.

Use Pythagorean Theorem: $a^2 + b^2 = c^2$

$x^2 + x^2 = 8^2 \Rightarrow 2x^2 = 8^2 \Rightarrow 2x^2 = 64 \Rightarrow x^2 = 32 \Rightarrow x = \sqrt{32}$

The area of the square is: $\sqrt{32} \times \sqrt{32} = 32$

20) Choice B is correct

$$\text{Probability} = \frac{\textit{number of desired outcomes}}{\text{number of total outcomes}} = \frac{18}{12+18+18+24} = \frac{18}{72} = \frac{1}{4}$$

21) Choices A and E are correct

(If you selected 3 choices and 2 of them are correct, then you get one point. If you answered 2 or 3 choices and one of them is correct, you receive one point. If you selected more than 3 choices, you won't get any point for this question.)

$x + 2y = 4$. Plug in the values of x and y from choices provided. Then:

☐A. $(-2, 3)$ $x + 2y = 4 \rightarrow -2 + 2(3) = 4 \rightarrow -2 + 6 = 4$ This is true!

☐B. $(1, 2)$ $x + 2y = 4 \rightarrow 1 + 2(2) = 4 \rightarrow 1 + 4 = 5$ This is NOT true!

☐C. $(-1, 3)$ $x + 2y = 4 \rightarrow -1 + 2(3) = 4 \rightarrow -1 + 6 = 5$ This is NOT true!

☐D. $(-3, 4)$ $x + 2y = 4 \rightarrow -3 + 2(4) = 4 \rightarrow -3 + 8 = 5$ This is NOT true!

☐E. $(0, 2)$ $x + 2y = 4 \rightarrow 0 + 2(2) = 4 \rightarrow 4 = 4$ This is true!

22) Choice A is correct

The width of the rectangle is twice its length. Let x be the length. Then, $width = 2x$

Perimeter of the rectangle is $2\ (width + length) = 2(2x + x) = 60 \Rightarrow 6x = 60 \Rightarrow x = 10$

Length of the rectangle is 10 meters.

23) Choice D is correct

$\text{average} = \frac{\text{sum of terms}}{\text{number of terms}} \Rightarrow$ (average of 6 numbers) $12 = \frac{\text{sum of numbers}}{6} \Rightarrow$sum of 6 numbers is $12 \times 6 = 72$

(average of 4 numbers) $10 = \frac{\text{sum of numbers}}{4} \Rightarrow$sum of 4 numbers is $10 \times 4 = 40$

$\textit{sum of } 6\ \textit{numbers} - \textit{sum of } 4\ \textit{numbers} = \textit{sum of } 2\ \textit{numbers}, 72 - 40 = 32,$

average of 2 numbers $= \frac{32}{2} = 16$

24) Choice C is correct

Solving Systems of Equations by Elimination

Multiply the first equation by (-2), then add it to the second equation.

$$\begin{array}{r} -2(2x+5y=\ 11) \\ 4x-2y=-14 \\ \hline \end{array} \Rightarrow \begin{array}{r} -4x-10y=\ -22 \\ 4x-2y=-14 \end{array} \Rightarrow -12y=\ -36 \Rightarrow y=\ 3$$

Plug in the value of y into one of the equations and solve for x.

$2x+5(3)=11 \Rightarrow 2x+15=11 \Rightarrow 2x=-4 \Rightarrow x=-2$

25) Choice B is correct

The perimeter of the trapezoid is $36\ cm$.

Therefore, the missing side (height) is = $36-8-12-6\ =10$

Area of a trapezoid: $A\ =\ \frac{1}{2}\ h\ (b_1+\ b_2)=\ \frac{1}{2}\ (10)\ (6\ +\ 8)\ =70$

26) Choice B is correct

The probability of choosing a Hearts is $\frac{13}{52}=\frac{1}{4}$

27) Choices D and E are correct

(If you selected 3 choices and 2 of them are correct, then you get one point. If you answered 2 or 3 choices and one of them is correct, you receive one point. If you selected more than 3 choices, you won't get any point for this question.)

First, find the sum of five numbers.

$$\text{average}\ =\frac{\text{sum of terms}}{\text{number of terms}} \Rightarrow\ 25=\frac{\text{sum of 5 numbers}}{5} \Rightarrow \text{sum of 5 numbers} = 25\times 5\ =125$$

The sum of 5 numbers is 125. If a sixth number that is greater than 42 is added to these numbers, then the sum of 6 numbers must be greater than 162. $125+42=167$

If the number was 42, then the average of the numbers is:

$$\text{average} = \frac{\text{sum of terms}}{\text{number of terms}}=\frac{167}{6}=27.83$$

Since the number is bigger than 42. Then, the average of six numbers must be greater than 27.83.

Choices D and E are greater than 27.83.

28) The answer is 28.

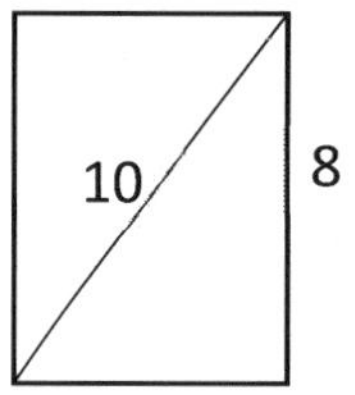

Let x be the width of the rectangle. Use Pythagorean Theorem:

$a^2+b^2=c^2$

$x^{\ 2}+\ 8^{\ 2}=10^2\ \Rightarrow x^{\ 2}+\ 64\ =100\ \Rightarrow\ x^{\ 2}=100-\ 64\ =\ 36\ \Rightarrow\ x\ =6$

Perimeter of the rectangle = $2\ (length\ +\ width)\ = 2\ (8\ +\ 6) = 2\ (14) = 28$

29) Choice C is correct

Th ratio of boy to girls is 4: 7. Therefore, there are 4 boys out of 11 students. To find the answer, first divide the total number of students by 11, then multiply the result by 4. $44\ \div\ 11 = 4 \Rightarrow$ $4 \times 4\ = 16$. There are 16 boys and 28 $(44 - 16)$ girls. So, 12 more boys should be enrolled to make the ratio 1: 1

30) Choice A is correct

2,500 out of 55,000 equals to $\frac{2500}{55000} = \frac{25}{550} = \frac{1}{22}$

31) The answer is 60.

Jason needs an 75% average to pass for five exams. Therefore, the sum of 5 exams must be at lease $5 \times 75 = 375$. The sum of 4 exams is: $68\ + 72 + 85\ +\ 90\ = 315$.

The minimum score Jason can earn on his fifth and final test to pass is: $375 - 315 = 60$

32) Choice D is correct

Isolate and solve for x. $\frac{2}{3}x + \frac{1}{6} = \frac{1}{3} \Rightarrow \frac{2}{3}x = \frac{1}{3} - \frac{1}{6} = \frac{1}{6} \Rightarrow \frac{2}{3}x = \frac{1}{6}$

Multiply both sides by the reciprocal of the coefficient of x. $(\frac{3}{2})\frac{2}{3}x = \frac{1}{6}(\frac{3}{2}) \Rightarrow x = \frac{3}{12} = \frac{1}{4}$

33) Choice B is correct

Use simple interest formula: $I = prt$ (I = interest, p = principal, r = rate, t = time)

$I = (12000)(0.035)(2) = 840$

34) Choice D is correct

Simplify. $6x^2y^3(2x^2y)^3 = 6x^2y^3(8x^6y^3) = 48x^8y^6$

35) Choice C is correct

Surface Area of a cylinder $= 2\pi r\ (r\ +\ h)$, The radius of the cylinder is $3\ (6 \div 2)$ inches and its height is 8 inches. Therefore, Surface Area of a cylinder $= 2\pi\ (3)\ (3\ +\ 8)\ \ = 66\ \pi$

36) Choice C is correct

The square of a number is $\frac{25}{64}$, then the number is the square root of $\frac{25}{64}$. $\sqrt{\frac{25}{64}} = \frac{5}{8}$

The cube of the number is: $(\frac{5}{8})^3 = \frac{125}{512}$

37) Choice B is correct

Write the numbers in order: $2, 19, 27, 28, 35, 44, 67$.

Median is the number in the middle. So, the median is 28.

38) The answer is 170.

Use the information provided in the question to draw the shape.

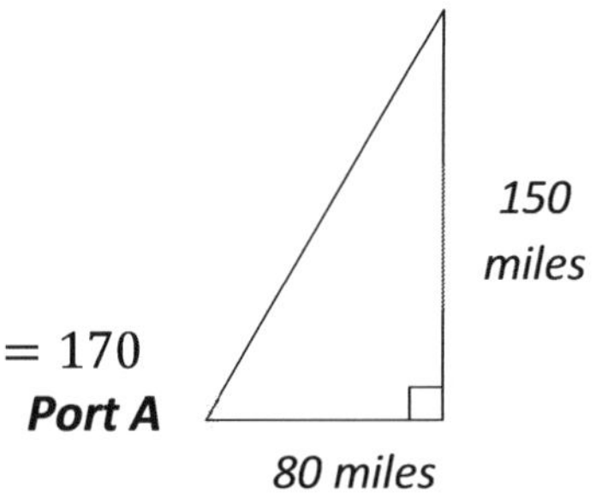

Use Pythagorean Theorem: $a^2 + b^2 = c^2$

$80^2 + 150^2 = c^2 \Rightarrow 6400 + 22500 = c^2 \Rightarrow 28900 = c^2 \Rightarrow c = 170$

39) Choice B is correct

Plug in 104 for F and then solve for C. $C = \frac{5}{9}(F - 32) \Rightarrow C = \frac{5}{9}(104 - 32) \Rightarrow$

$C = \frac{5}{9}(72) = 40$

40) Choice C is correct

Let x be the number. Write the equation and solve for x. $40\%\ of\ x = 4 \Rightarrow 0.40\,x = 4 \Rightarrow x = 4 \div 0.40 = 10$

41) Choice D is correct

Let x be all expenses, then $\frac{22}{100}x = \$660 \rightarrow x = \frac{100 \times \$660}{22} = \$3{,}000$. He spent for his rent: $\frac{27}{100} \times \$3{,}000 = \$810$

42) Choice C is correct

The distance between Jason and Joe is 9 miles. Jason running at 5.5 miles per hour and Joe is running at the speed of 7 miles per hour. Therefore, every hour the distance is 1.5 miles less.

$9 \div 1.5 = 6$

43) Choice D is correct

The failing rate is 11 out of $55 = \frac{11}{55}$. Change the fraction to percent: $\frac{11}{55} \times 100\% = 20\%$

20 percent of students failed. Therefore, 80 percent of students passed the exam.

44) Choice A is correct

First, find the number. Let x be the number. Write the equation and solve for x.

150% of a number is 75, then: $1.5 \times x = 75 \Rightarrow x = 75 \div 1.5 = 50$

90% of 50 is: $0.9 \times 50 = 45$

45) The answer is 2.

Solve for y. $4x - 2y = 6 \Rightarrow -2y = 6 - 4x \Rightarrow y = 2x - 3$. The slope of the line is 2.

46) Choice A is correct

Let x be the number of new shoes the team can purchase. Therefore, the team can purchase $120\ x$. The team had \$20,000 and spent \$14,000. Now the team can spend on new shoes \$6,000 at most. Now, write the inequality: $120x + 14{,}000 \ \leq 20{,}000$

Mathematical Reasoning Practice Test 2

Answers and Explanations

1) Choice B is correct

In scientific notation all numbers are written in the form of: $m \times 10^n$, where m is between 1 and 10. To find an equivalent value of 0.000 000 000 000 042 121, move the decimal point to the right so that you have a number that is between 1 and 10. Then: 4.2121
Now, determine how many places the decimal moved in step 1, then put it as the power of 10. We moved the decimal point 14 places. Then: 10^{-14} → When the decimal moved to the right, the exponent is negative. Then: $0.000\ 000\ 000\ 000\ 042\ 121 = 4.2121 \times 10^{-14}$

2) Choice D is correct

Let x be the integer. Then: $2x - 5 = 83$. Add 5 both sides: $2x = 88$, Divide both sides by 2:

$$x = 44$$

3) Choice D is correct

To find the discount, multiply the number by $(100\% - rate\ of\ discount)$.

Therefore, for the first discount we get: $(200)\ (100\% - 15\%) = (200)(0.85) = 170$

For the next 15% discount: $(200)(0.85)(0.85)$

4) Choice B is correct

Plug in each pair of number in the equation:

A. $(2,1)$: $2\,(2) + 4\,(1) = 8$
B. $(-1,3)$: $2\,(-1) + 4\,(3) = 10$
C. $(-2,2)$: $2\,(-2) + 4\,(2) = 4$
D. $(2,2)$: $2\,(2) + 4\,(2) = 12$

Only choice B is correct.

5) The answer is: -30

Use PEMDAS (order of operation):

$5 + 8 \times (-2) - [4 + 22 \times 5] \div 6 = 5 + 8 \times (-2) - [4 + 110] \div 6$
$= 5 + 8 \times (-2) - [114] \div 6 = 5 + (-16) - 19 = 5 + (-16) - 19$
$= -11 - 19 = -30$

6) Choice C is correct

85% of 40 is: $85\% \; of \; 40 = 0.85 \times 40 = 34$. So, the student solves 34 questions correctly.

7) Choice D is correct

If the length of the box is 27, then the width of the box is one third of it, 9, and the height of the box is 3 (one third of the width). The volume of the box is: $V = lwh = (27)(9)(3) = 729$

8) Choice C is correct

Write the equation and solve for B: $0.60 A = 0.30 B$, divide both sides by 0.30, then:

$\frac{0.60}{0.30} A = B$, therefore: $B = 2A$, and B is 2 times of A or it's 200% of A.

9) The answer is 90.

To find the number of possible outfit combinations, multiply number of options for each factor:

$6 \times 3 \times 5 = 90$

10) Choice D is correct

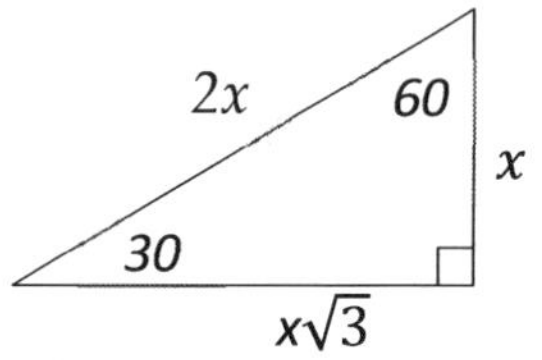

The relationship among all sides of special right triangle

$30° - 60° - 90°$ is provided in this triangle:

In this triangle, the opposite side of $30°$ angle is half of the hypotenuse.

Draw the shape for this question:

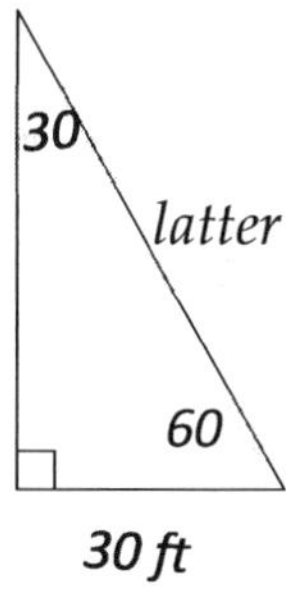

The latter is the hypotenuse. Therefore, the latter is $60 \; ft$.

11) Choice C is correct

Let x be the number. Write the equation and solve for x. $(24 - x) \div x = 3$. Multiply both sides by x. $(24 - x) = 3x$, then add x both sides. $24 = 4x$, now divide both sides by 4. $x = 6$

12) Choice B is correct

The sum of supplement angles is 180. Let x be that angle. Therefore, $x + 5x = 180$. $6 = 180$, divide both sides by 6: $x = 30$

13) Choice C is correct

The average speed of john is: $150 \div 6 = 25 \; km$, The average speed of Alice is: $180 \div 4 = 45 \; km$. Write the ratio and simplify. $25 : 45 \Rightarrow 5 : 9$

14) Choice A is correct

The percent of girls playing tennis is: $40\% \times 25\% = 0.40 \times 0.25 = 0.10 = 10\%$

15) The answer is -5.

Solving Systems of Equations by Elimination

$$\begin{aligned} 3x - 4y &= -40 \\ -x + 2y &= 10 \end{aligned}$$

Multiply the second equation by 3, then add it to the first equation.

$$\begin{aligned} 3x - 4y &= -40 \\ 3(-x + 2y &= 10) \end{aligned} \Rightarrow \begin{aligned} 3x - 4y &= -40 \\ -3x + 6y &= 30) \end{aligned} \Rightarrow 2y = -10 \Rightarrow y = -5$$

16) Choice C is correct

Add the first 5 numbers. $40 + 45 + 50 + 35 + 55 = 225$. To find the distance traveled in the next 5 hours, multiply the average by number of hours. $Distance = Average \times Rate = 50 \times 5 = 250$. Add both numbers. $250 + 225 = 475$

17) Choice C is correct

Use distance formula: $Distance = Rate \times time \Rightarrow 420 = 50 \times T$, divide both sides by 50. $420 \div 50 = T \Rightarrow T = 8.4\ hours$.

Change hours to minutes for the decimal part. $0.4\ hours = 0.4 \times 60 = 24\ minutes$.

18) Choices C and E are correct

(If you selected 3 choices and 2 of them are correct, then you get one point. If you answered 2 or 3 choices and one of them is correct, you receive one point. If you selected more than 3 choices, you won't get any point for this question.)

The ratio of red marbles to blue marbles is 2: 5. Therefore, total number of marbles must be divisible by 7: $2 + 5 = 7$. Let's review the choices:

☐A. 324: $324 \div 7 = 46.28 \ldots$

☐B. 688: $688 \div 7 = 98.28 \ldots$

☐C. 826 $826 \div 7 = 118$

☐D. 596 $596 \div 7 = 85.14 \ldots$

☐E. 658 $658 \div 7 = 94$

Only choices C and E when divided by 7 result a whole number.

19) Choices C and D are correct

(If you selected 3 choices and 2 of them are correct, then you get one point. If you answered 2 or 3 choices and one of them is correct, you receive one point. If you selected more than 3 choices, you won't get any point for this question.)

$3x + 2y = 11$. Plug in the values of x and y from choices provided. Then:

☐A. $(-1,3)$ $3x+2y=11 \rightarrow 3(-1)+2(3)=11 \rightarrow -3+6=11$ NOT true!

☐B. $(2,3)$ $3x+2y=11 \rightarrow 3(2)+2(3)=11 \rightarrow 6+6=11$ NOT true!

☐C. $(-1,7)$ $3x+2y=11 \rightarrow 3(-1)+2(7)=11 \rightarrow -3+14=11$ Bingo!

☐D. $(5,-2)$ $3x+2y=11 \rightarrow 3(5)+2(-2)=11 \rightarrow 15-4=11$ Yes!

☐E. $(0,2)$ $3x+2y=11 \rightarrow 3(0)+2(2)=11 \rightarrow 0+4=11$ Nope!

20) Choice D is correct

Use Pythagorean Theorem: $a^2+b^2=c^2, 6^2 + 8^2 = c^2 \Rightarrow 100 = c^2 \Rightarrow c = 10$

21) The answer is 240.

Th ratio of boy to girls is 2: 3. Therefore, there are 2 boys out of 5 students. To find the answer, first divide the total number of students by 5, then multiply the result by 2.

$600 \div 5 = 120 \Rightarrow 120 \times 2 = 240$

22) Choice C is correct

Use percent formula: $\text{part} = \frac{\text{percent}}{100} \times \text{whole}$

$25 = \frac{percent}{100} \times 20 \Rightarrow 25 = \frac{percent \times 20}{100} \Rightarrow 25 = \frac{percent \times 2}{10}$, multiply both sides by 10.
$250 = percent \times 2$, divide both sides by 2. $125 = percent$

23) The answer is 130.

The perimeter of the trapezoid is 54.

Therefore, the missing side (height) is $= 54 - 18 - 12 - 14 = 10$

Area of a trapezoid: $A = \frac{1}{2} h (b_1 + b_2) = \frac{1}{2}(10)(12+14) = 130$

24) Choice C is correct

Let x be the number. Write the equation and solve for x.

$\frac{2}{3} \times 18 = \frac{2}{5} . x \Rightarrow \frac{2 \times 18}{3} = \frac{2x}{5}$, use cross multiplication to solve for x.

$5 \times 36 = 2x \times 3 \Rightarrow 180 = 6x \Rightarrow x = 30$

25) Choice B is correct

To find the discount, multiply the number by $(100\% - rate\ of\ discount)$.

Therefore, for the first discount we get: $(D)\ (100\% - 20\%) = (D)(0.80) = 0.80\ D$

For increase of 10%: $(0.80\ D)(100\% + 10\%) = (0.80D)(1.10) = 0.88\ D = 88\%\ of\ D$

26) Choice B is correct

Use the formula of areas of circles.

$Area = \pi r^2 \Rightarrow 64\pi = \pi r^2 \Rightarrow 64 = r^2 \Rightarrow r = 8$

Radius of the circle is 8. Now, use the circumference formula:

Circumference $= 2\pi r = 2\pi\ (8) = 16\pi$

27) Choice B is correct

Use the formula for Percent of Change. $\frac{\text{New Value}-\text{Old Value}}{Old\ Value} \times 100\ \%$

$\frac{28-40}{40} \times 100\% = -30\%$ (negative sign here means that the new price is less than old price).

28) Choice A is correct

Let x be the number of years. Therefore, \$2,000 per year equals $2000x$. starting from \$24,000 annual salary means you should add that amount to $2000x$. Income more than that is:

$I > 2000x + 24000$

29) Choice C is correct

The question is this: 1.75 is what percent of 1.25? Use percent formula:

$\text{part} = \frac{\text{percent}}{100} \times \text{whole} \Rightarrow 1.75 = \frac{percent}{100} \times 1.25 \Rightarrow 1.75 = \frac{percent \times 1.25}{100} \Rightarrow$

$175 = percent \times 1.25 \Rightarrow percent = \frac{175}{1.25} = 140$

30) Choice B is correct

Use the information provided in the question to draw the shape.

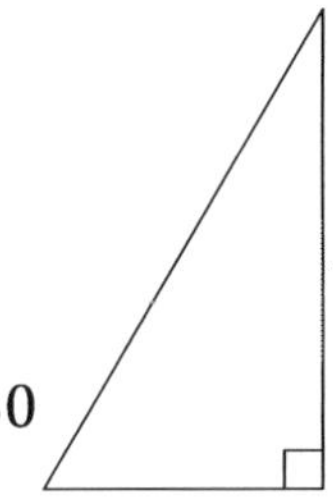

Use Pythagorean Theorem: $a^2 + b^2 = c^2$

$40^2 + 30^2 = c^2 \Rightarrow 1600 + 900 = c^2 \Rightarrow 2500 = c^2 \Rightarrow c = 50$

31) Choice D is correct

Some of prime numbers are: $2, 3, 5, 7, 11, 13$

Find the product of two consecutive prime numbers: $2 \times 3 = 6$ (not in the options)

$3 \times 5 = 15$ (bingo!), $5 \times 7 = 35$ (not in the options)

32) Choice B is correct

The question is this: 529.72 is what percent of 646? Use percent formula:

$part = \frac{percent}{100} \times whole. \qquad 529.72 = \frac{percent}{100} \times 646 \Rightarrow 529.72 = \frac{percent \times 646}{100} \Rightarrow$

$529.72 = percent \times 646 \Rightarrow percent = \frac{529.72}{646} = 82$

529.72 is 82% of 646. Therefore, the discount is: $100\% - 82\% = 18\%$

33) Choice B is correct

If the score of Mia was 40, therefore the score of Ava is 20. Since, the score of Emma was half as that of Ava, therefore, the score of Emma is 10.

34) Choice D is correct

If 17 balls are removed from the bag at random, there will be one ball in the bag. The probability of choosing a brown ball is 1 out of 18. Therefore, the probability of not choosing a brown ball is 17 out of 18 and the probability of having not a brown ball after removing 17 balls is the same.

35) Choice B is correct

Let x be the smallest number. Then, these are the numbers: $x, x+1, x+2, x+3, x+4$

$$\text{average} = \frac{\text{sum of terms}}{\text{number of terms}} \Rightarrow 38 = \frac{x+(x+1)+(x+2)+(x+3)+(x+4)}{5} \Rightarrow 38 = \frac{5x+10}{5} \Rightarrow$$

$190 = 5x + 10 \Rightarrow 180 = 5x \Rightarrow x = 36$

36) Choice D is correct

The area of the floor is: $8\ cm \times 24\ cm = 192\ cm^2$. The number of tiles needed $=$

$$192 \div 8 = 24$$

37) Choice C is correct

The weight of 12.2 meters of this rope is: $12.2 \times 600\ g = 7320\ g$

$1\ kg = 1000\ g$, therefore, $7320\ g \div 1000 = 7.32\ kg$

38) Choice C is correct

4% of the volume of the solution is alcohol. Let x be the volume of the solution.

Then: $4\%\ of\ x = 32\ ml \Rightarrow 0.04\,x = 32 \Rightarrow x = 32 \div 0.04 = 800$

39) Choice B is correct

$\text{average} = \frac{\text{sum of terms}}{\text{number of terms}}$. The sum of the weight of all girls is: $23 \times 60 = 1{,}380\ kg$, The sum of the weight of all boys is: $32 \times 62 = 1984\ kg$. The sum of the weight of all students is: $1{,}380 + 1{,}984 = 3{,}364\ kg$. $\quad average = \frac{3364}{55} = 61.16$

40) Choice D is correct

Let x be the original price. If the price of a laptop is decreased by 20% to $\$360$, then:

$80\%\ of\ x = 360 \Rightarrow 0.80x = 360 \Rightarrow x = 360 \div 0.80 = 450$

41) Choice B is correct

Write the numbers in order: $3, 5, 8, 10, 13, 15, 19$

Since we have 7 numbers (7 is odd), then the median is the number in the middle, which is 10.

42) The answer is 678.24.

Surface Area of a cylinder $= 2\pi r(r + h)$, The radius of the cylinder is 6 inches and its height is 12 inches. π is about 3.14. Then: Surface Area of a cylinder $= 2(\pi)(6)(6 + 12) = 216\,\pi = 678.24$

43) The answer is 12.

$$average = \frac{sum\ of\ terms}{number\ of\ terms} \Rightarrow 15 = \frac{13 + 15 + 20 + x}{4} \Rightarrow 60 = 48 + x \Rightarrow x = 12$$

44) Choice C is correct

Let x be the original price. If the price of the sofa is decreased by 25% to \$420, then:
$75\%\ of\ x = 420 \Rightarrow 0.75x = 420 \Rightarrow x = 420 \div 0.75 = 560$

45) Choice D and E are correct

(If you selected 3 choices and 2 of them are correct, then you get one point. If you answered 2 or 3 choices and one of them is correct, you receive one point. If you selected more than 3 choices, you won't get any point for this question.)

The equation of a line is in the form of $y = mx + b$, where m is the slope of the line and b is the $y - intercept$ of the line. Two points $(1, 2)$ and $(-1, 6)$ are on line A. Therefore, the slope of the line A is: $slope\ of\ line\ A = \frac{y_2 - y_1}{x_2 - x_1} = \frac{6-2}{-1-1} = \frac{4}{-2} = -2$

The slope of line A is -2. Thus, the formula of the line A is: $y = mx + b = -2x + b$, choose a point and plug in the values of x and y in the equation to solve for b. Let's choose point $(1, 2)$. Then: $y = -2x + b \rightarrow 2 = -2(1) + b \rightarrow b = 2 + 2 = 4$. The equation of line A is: $y = -2x + 4$

Now, let's review the choices provided:

A. $(-1, 2)$ $y = -2x + 4 \rightarrow 2 = -2(-1) + 4 = 6$ This is not true.

B. $(5, 7)$ $y = -2x + 4 \rightarrow 7 = -2(5) + 4 = -6$ This is not true.

C. $(3, 4)$ $y = -2x + 4 \rightarrow 4 = -2(3) + 4 = -2$ This is not true.

D. $(3, -2)$ $y = -2x + 4 \rightarrow -2 = -2(3) + 4 = -2$ This is true!

E. $(6, -8)$ $y = -2x + 4 \rightarrow -8 = -2(6) + 4 = -8$ This is true!

46) Choice C is correct

Use simple interest formula: $I = prt$ ($I = interest, p = principal, r = rate, t = time$)

$I = (9{,}000)(0.045)(5) = 2{,}025$

"Effortless Math Education" Publications

Effortless Math authors' team strives to prepare and publish the best quality GED Mathematics learning resources to make learning Math easier for all. We hope that our publications help you learn Math in an effective way and prepare for the GED test.

We all in Effortless Math wish you good luck and successful studies!

Effortless Math Authors

Made in the USA
San Bernardino, CA
07 February 2020

64140680R00098